Biblical ABCs

Biblical ABCs

The Basics of Christian Resistance

Translated by
Eleonora Hof and Collin Cornell

LEXINGTON BOOKS/FORTRESS ACADEMIC
Lanham • Boulder • New York • London

Published by Lexington Books/Fortress Academic
Lexington Books is an imprint of The Rowman & Littlefield Publishing Group, Inc.
4501 Forbes Boulevard, Suite 200, Lanham, Maryland 20706
www.rowman.com

86-90 Paul Street, London EC2A 4NE, United Kingdom

Copyright © 2022 by The Rowman & Littlefield Publishing Group, Inc.

All rights reserved. No part of this book may be reproduced in any form or by any electronic or mechanical means, including information storage and retrieval systems, without written permission from the publisher, except by a reviewer who may quote passages in a review.

British Library Cataloguing in Publication Information Available

Library of Congress Cataloging-in-Publication Data

Names: Miskotte, K. H. (Kornelis Heiko), 1894–1976, author. | Hof, Eleonora, 1986–, translator. | Cornell, Collin, 1988–, translator.
Title: Biblical ABCs : the basics of Christian resistance / by K.H. Miskotte ; translated by Eleonora Hof and Collin Cornell.
Other titles: Bijbels ABC. English
Description: Lanham, Maryland : Lexington Books/Fortress Academic, [2021] | Includes bibliographical references and index. | Summary: "Biblical ABCs is a theological resistance primer. Written illegally under Nazi occupation by Dutch pastor and theologian Kornelis Heiko (K.H.) Miskotte, it provides basic biblical coordinates for Christians seeking to live bold and faithful lives in times of crisis, alienation, and alternative facts"—Provided by publisher.
Identifiers: LCCN 2021034106 (print) | LCCN 2021034107 (ebook) | ISBN 9781978707535 (cloth) | ISBN 9781978707542 (epub)
Subjects: LCSH: Bible—Criticism, interpretation, etc.
Classification: LCC BS538 .M5513 2021 (print) | LCC BS538 (ebook) | DDC 220.6—dc23
LC record available at https://lccn.loc.gov/2021034106
LC ebook record available at https://lccn.loc.gov/2021034107

Contents

Miskotte's Foreword to the 1941 Edition — vii
Translators' Preface — ix
Introduction by Rinse Reeling Brouwer — xv

1 Reading Scripture — 1
2 Teaching — 7
3 Name — 17
4 The Names of God — 27
5 The Order of God's Virtues — 35
6 The Unity of God's Virtues — 45
7 The Acts — 57
8 Word — 67
9 Way — 77
10 Sanctification — 87
11 Expectation — 109
12 The Life of Community — 133

Appendix: Log of Additions to the 1941 Edition — 151
Bibliography — 155

Scripture Index 159

Author Index 169

About the Authors and Translators 171

Miskotte's Foreword to the 1941 Edition

In Amsterdam, as in other places of our fatherland this summer, new small groups have formed for communal Bible study with housemates, neighbors, and community members; in Amsterdam this movement was initiated by the Council of Reverends. Before the institution and organization of these small groups, a course was being offered for those willing to conduct small groups, and this course is still ongoing from week to week in the city center, the New Church on Dam Square. It seemed necessary to us that this course, which discusses a given Bible passage together with "small group leaders," should follow a general introduction concerning the *grondlijnen*, ground-lines, of Holy Scripture.

This task was assigned to me.

The publisher thought it would be a service to many to turn the content of this general course into a small book.

Here it is; as preliminary and simple, demanding and impatient as it was and as it, according to us, must be.

We have no time to lose. I would like to quietly write a book in lofty prose, to venture further from the coast and descend into the deep. But everything has its appointed time; and the times differ, their pace and purpose vary.

There is so much to catch up and make good and set right. And preferably soon.

Let everybody then take what serves them and do something with it in their lives, for themselves and for others, for the church and for the people of these lands. Let no one embolden themselves in these times to draw too sharp a line between churchly and unchurched people, all the more if they know what churchly instruction really is.

One should refrain from looking here for a pocket-sized dogmatics, or even a layperson's dogmatics. It is and it remains *formal*; it helps to understand *the language of the Bible*. If through this introduction the Bible's most important contents are coming to light, and even, yes, people are taking actual decisions for their spiritual life, all this is not due to our booklet but belongs, rather, to the particularities of the Book-of-Books.

That the Old Testament is the starting point for our considerations does not of course mean we prefer the promise over the fulfillment; it results instead from the focus of this booklet on the *language* of Scripture, and the language of the New Testament finds its roots utterly and completely in the Old.

We must as a community get to work to gain knowledge and to live again, and better, from out of that knowledge, to live "under the Word."

Wholeness to the reader! Blessings to the doer!

K.H.M.
Autumn 1941

Translators' Preface

We are writing this preface in the days after January 6, 2021—the day when armed supporters of Donald J. Trump breached the US Capitol building to interrupt Congress's certification of the election of his presidential rival and successor. Many first-hand accounts of the uprising have been published. Cellphone videos circulated widely online. All these sources show that this was *a Christian event*. Proud Boys—members of a white supremacist paramilitary—knelt in prayer. People raised a cross. Someone yelled out, "shout if you love Jesus!" and then, after the crowd cheered: "shout if you love Trump!" (to which the response was even louder).[1]

It was also and at the same time a demonstration of white power, white violence, and white impunity. Nazi and white-supremacist paraphernalia proliferated.[2] Black Capitol Police officers suffered a cascade of racist slurs. The man at the center of the event, who had incited the crowds that morning, has become a de facto symbol of white, patriarchal primacy. He released a video late on the 6th professing to the mob, "we love you, you're very special."

The day disturbs us in a variety of ways, and its overall historical significance—as a turning point? a harbinger?—is yet unknown. But as Christian theologians, it is this one aspect of the episode in particular that demands our energies: the fusion of the Good News about Jesus Christ into *Herrenvolk* ideology. Teasing these two apart, and finding resources within the Christian faith to oppose white supremacy, is a theological project that we have been pursuing for some time. In fact there is a certain (awful) symmetry to our completing this translation at this moment, because we began it in the aftermath of Charlottesville—the Unite the Right march on August 11 and

12, 2017, when neo-Nazis marched through the streets of Charlottesville, Virginia, chanting "Jews will not replace us."

Eleonora had given a presentation earlier that year (in April 2017) at a conference in Groningen. She was at that time a research fellow at the Protestant Theological University in Amsterdam, having completed her PhD in postcolonial missiology there in 2016. The title of her conference paper was "Resistance in the Work of K.H. Miskotte." In it, she told how the Dutch pastor Miskotte *theologized* against Nazism and how he *practiced resistance* to it, both before the war and during it. When Eleonora uploaded the paper to an academic website, Collin, then a PhD student in Hebrew Bible at Emory University, read it and wrote to Eleonora. In that initial email message, he said:

> I think you are right that Miskotte's thoroughly anti-pagan approach to theology, grounded in the Name of God, is of urgent contemporary interest. What is happening in the United States right now is not so different, I don't think, from what occurred in Germany in the 1930s: theologically speaking, white evangelicals have utterly lost the ability to distinguish between their own ethnic interests and ethno-culture and the good news of the Christian faith. I came to Miskotte through Karl Barth on one side and Brevard Childs on the other. I love the particularity and Christocentrism of Barth's theology on the one hand, and Childs's insistence on the canonicity of the [Old Testament] on the other. But I could not yet find a way to hold these interests together with a strong critical stance towards the identification of the gospel and a particular culture—until, I am discerning, I have found Miskotte.

We had both started our theological existence as translators—Bible translators, or at least, would-be Bible translators. Although we never met while we were there, we interned at roughly the same time in Kathmandu with the Summer Institute of Linguistics (SIL), a nonprofit that supports Bible translation work. Afterwards, inspired and challenged by our internship experience, we each pursued master's degrees, Eleonora one in Bible Translation at the Vrije Universiteit in Amsterdam and Collin an MDiv at Princeton Theological Seminary. Our subsequent academic pursuits diverged. But our interest in translation never subsided, and so it was that rather shortly after beginning our correspondence, Eleonora proposed that we translate Miskotte's *Bijbels ABC*. This was, in retrospect, audacious on several fronts: Miskotte is a well-known and abidingly influential theologian in the Netherlands, so the stakes were (and are) high. His Dutch is now old-fashioned, also quite sinuous, and Collin had little-to-no Dutch to start with. And, too, our own lives changed very much over the following years.

OUR APPROACH TO TRANSLATION

We faced significant translation decisions right away. The first concerned which edition of the book to use as our base text. The first edition from 1941 is spare, urgent, and raw. The second edition from after the war (1966) is slightly more expansive and explanatory, and it reflects Miskotte's deepening engagement with nihilism. In view of our own situation, of a galvanizing far-right, we felt a greater kinship with the intensity of Miskotte's original and a greater distance from his postwar musings on nihilism. In consequence, we chose to use the 1941 edition, though we referred constantly to Hinrich Stoevesandt's 1976 translation into German, itself based on the 1966 edition; and at a few points, logged in our appendix, we decided that Miskotte's later emendations provided helpful clarification, and we kept them.[3]

A second, early decision pertained to the main title of the book. In Dutch, *Bijbels ABC* is singular: Biblical ABC. But in American English, the noun is always plural, ABCs (sometimes written, inexplicably, with an apostrophe: ABC's). Given Miskotte's theological emphasis on unity—already in chapter 1 he puts THE UNITY of Scripture in uppercase, and he dedicates chapter 6 to the unity of God's virtues—it might seem confusing to make a plural noun the title and organizing concept of the book. But in fact, we discerned that this was simply a case of accommodating the target language. American English has no other option, and besides, the plural of ABCs identifies a singular entity (the series of letters that comprise the alphabet).

Another and more freighted issue we deliberated about is gendered language. In Miskotte's original, both God and humanity receive consistently masculine pronouns. This was, of course, not just commonplace but ubiquitous in 1941 (and 1966). Here, too, however, the target language pressed upon us. Recent English-language theology avoids gendering God and even moreso gendering humankind at large. Theologically constructive works—texts that make "live" arguments about the activity and profile of God and do not only register observations about classic antecedents—are especially careful to observe this gender neutrality. By following suit, we signal with our translation a constructive purpose: we intend this book as a *proposal*, as *instruction*, and not as *historical exercise*.

So, too, we found reasons within Miskotte's own thinking to support this nongendered use. The Name of God, in all its particularity and concreteness, is the radial point of Miskotte's theology, "the A of the biblical ABCs" (see chapter 3). In its specificity, the Name interrupts all received, default, "self-evident" divine attributes. We cannot know *a priori* who or what God is, nor can we simply assume the attributes that have been handed down to us, of impassibility, omnipotence, omnipresence. In the same way, the Name calls into question the prevailing theological habit of masculine reference; only tracing out the Name, spelling the ABCs, will show whether and to what extent masculinity is a relevant category for speaking about God. Our translation hence replaces all masculine pronouns (He, Him, His) with God, "God's self," or "One." In our judgment, the substitution of "Him" with "One" (or: "this One") fits the character of Miskotte's thinking quite well, since it amplifies the irreplaceable singularity of the Name.

A final challenge of translating Miskotte is his history of reception in the Netherlands. Certain terms that he uses in *Biblical ABCs* came to have a technical meaning in the theological discourse of his aftercomers like Frans Breukelman or Karel Deurloo. Miskotte uses a cluster of words built from the Dutch root *grond*, cognate to English "ground": *grondwoord*, *grondbestek*, *grondstructuur*, *grondpatroon*, *grondtaal*, *grondvorm*, *grondterm*, *grondbetekenis*, *grondgedachte*, *grondkarakter*. These terms indicate the biblical concepts which, according to Miskotte, scaffold the entirety of Scripture, and indeed, which organize this book, *Biblical ABCs*. Breukelman was Miskotte's student and, in some regards, his theological heir; his "*debarim*-studies" (word-studies) develop the link with specific Hebrew vocabulary even more directly.[4] The role of these *grondwoorden* became a distinguishing feature of the "Amsterdam School" of theology that arose in Miskotte's wake.

German can leverage the same root, *Grund*, to generate a web of similar words, and Stoevesandt's translation does just this. The trouble is that no satisfactory English equivalent for such words exists. They have been translated into English before; John Doberstein's translation of Miskotte's book *When the Gods are Silent* regularly mentions "basic words": "The basic words are the core of the Message. The structure of the whole ... continues to be determined by these basic words."[5] But this rendering flattens and obscures the technical quality of Miskotte's usage. In order to make the acute and programmatic character of these terms visible to English-language readers, we decided to leave them in italicized Dutch and then to give a rough calque: ground-word, ground-structure, ground-pattern, and so on. We hope this creates something of the impression of other theological loanwords, usually borrowed from German: *Sitz im Leben*, *Heilsgeschichte*. The foreignness of such terms foregrounds the particularity of their meaning. The same applies to *oerwoorden*, which appears in chapter 5 and at the end of chapter 10 and throughout chapter 11. German has the prefix *Ur-* ready to hand and can hence say *Urwort*. We have left the Dutch in italics and then glossed it with "primary word(s)."

One last instance where the Dutch history of reception has no ready-made English counterpart: the institution of the *leerhuis*. The term most literally means "learn(ing)-house" or "house of learning." It is cognate to the German *Lehrhaus* and translates the Hebrew *beit midrash*, a millennia-long Jewish school for Torah study housed at a synagogue or yeshiva. In Germany and the Netherlands, however, the *leerhuis*/*Lehrhaus* has a different currency.

The prominent Jewish thinker and theologian, Franz Rosenzweig, founded the *Freie Jüdische Lehrhaus* (Free Jewish House of Learning) in Frankfurt am Main in 1920. It originally served secularized, well-educated German Jews who wished to strengthen their Jewish identity. The study of Scripture (Tanak) in Hebrew was at the heart of its study program. As early as 1941, Miskotte initiated a *leerhuis* for Dutch Christians. It, too, focused on Hebrew Scripture, and it invited Jewish scholars, rabbis, and ordinary people into dialogue with Christians about biblical and theological topics. In this form, the interfaith institution gained some popularity, and at one time such houses of learning numbered in the hundreds across the Netherlands (also in Germany). Although their reach has receded since their high point in the 1960s and 1970s, and their participants have aged, the phenomenon of the *leerhuis/Lehrhaus* is familiar to Dutch and German readers in a way that it is not to Americans (or British). Since "house of learning" calls almost nothing to mind for English-speakers, we have opted to replace it with Hebrew *beit midrash*, which at least has the virtue of signaling a Jewish institution. We wish that such houses of learning might proliferate in Anglophone contexts, too.

In conclusion, we hope above all that our translation will instruct English-speaking Christians in the biblical ABCs; that it gives them a framework from which to understand the Bible. "This book is," as Miskotte says, "a linguistic inventory of the teaching, the holy instruction." As such, its concern is formal ("we do not attend to the content of the teaching, but only to its language and form of teaching"). And yet, attention to the form presses the reader beyond the formal. This is especially and emphatically the case when the entirety of Scripture is, as Miskotte alleges, anti-pagan testimony. In and of itself, Scripture subjects the default and dominant commitments of church and culture to fundamental critique. We pray therefore that our work will bolster Christians in their resistance to the deeply rooted and freshly ascendant power of white supremacy. We also intend for this translation to reawaken interest among English-language students, pastors, and theologians in the legacy of K.H. Miskotte.

We thank the Miskotte Foundation for providing us with the 1941 Dutch text, for permission to publish the photograph of Miskotte on the cover, and for all their support. All biblical quotes are taken from the New Revised Standard Version, except where noted.

NOTES

1. See Emma Green, "A Christian Insurrection," *The Atlantic*, Jan. 8, 2021, https://www.theatlantic.com/politics/archive/2021/01/evangelicals-catholics-jericho-march-capitol/617591; Sarah Posner, "How the Christian Right Helped Foment

Insurrection," *Rolling Stone,* Jan. 31, 2021, https://www.rollingstone.com/culture/culture-features/capitol-christian-right-trump-1121236.

2. Mallory Simon and Sarah Sidner, "Decoding the extremist symbols and groups at the Capitol Hill insurrection," CNN, Jan. 11, 2011; https://www.cnn.com/2021/01/09/us/capitol-hill-insurrection-extremist-flags-soh/index.html.

3. K.H. Miskotte, *Biblisches ABC: Wider das unbiblische Bibellesen*, trans. Hinrich Stoevesandt (Neurkirch-Vluyn: Neukirchener Verlag, 1976).

4. Frans Breukelman, *Debharim: der biblische Wirklichkeitsbegriff des Seins in der Tat*, Biblische Theologie II/1 (Kampen: Kok, 1998).

5. K.H. Miskotte, *When the Gods are Silent*, trans. John W. Doberstein (New York: Harper and Row, 1967), 192.

Introduction

Rinse Reeling Brouwer

In the early nocturnal hours of May 10, 1940, the German *Wehrmacht* invaded the Netherlands, Belgium, and Luxembourg. Dutch troops resisted for several days, but the bombardment of the city of Rotterdam compelled the government to capitulate on May 15. Two days later, Hitler proclaimed a decree by which he appointed the Austrian Nazi Arthur Seyss-Inquart as the *Reichskommissar* for the occupied territories of the Netherlands. In the beginning, the German administration tried to pacify the Dutch people "decently" as a "Germanic *Brudervolk*," and with some success. Many (too many!) officials, for example, complied with the first measures of Nazification such as signing the *Arierparagraph* for civil servants. However, in the autumn of 1940 the first protests arose. At Leiden University, R.P. Cleveringa, dean of the Faculty of Law, publicly contested the dismissal of his teacher and colleague, the Dutchman of Jewish origin E.M. Meijers,[1] and the students called for a strike. Jan Koopmans, reverend of the Dutch Reformed Church in Amsterdam, wrote an anonymous pamphlet *Bijna te laat!* (*Almost too late!*)[2] to warn the many that had already signed the first antisemitic declaration of the *Arierparagraph*. This pamphlet was published illegally and distributed by the so-called *Lunterse kring*, a group of persons from the church that had maintained relations with the Confessing Church in Nazi Germany during the thirties.[3]

A second pamphlet by the same underground group was published in Amsterdam and its environment after the strike at the end of February 1941; in spite of the Molotov-Ribbentrop pact, the strike was organized mainly by communist working men in protest of the Nazis' first anti-Jewish raid. The anonymous author was a friend and colleague of Koopmans, Kornelis Heiko Miskotte—although stylistically his text was much too easy to identify and so required radical revision by other members of the underground group. Its title was *Betere weerstand* (*Better Resistance*), and it was meant to warn against an activist demonstration of anti-German feelings because of only injured national pride.[4] Instead, it urged the importance of knowing the spiritual grounds for resistance and the indispensability of values such as justice and the search for humanity against the totalitarian state. It may be that the title of Miskotte's work had been inspired by the same expression (*bessere Widerstand*) that Karl Barth used in his letter of October 1940 to the Protestants in France.[5]

As pastors of the Dutch Reformed Congregation in the capital of the country, Koopmans and Miskotte felt obliged to contribute to this better resistance of the population. Remarkably, it was a grassroots movement for Bible reading that gave them the opportunity. In 1966, Miskotte remembered that a sudden asking after the sense of the Bible had taken place in 1940, and a movement arose among laypersons (housemates, neighbors) to read the Bible in common. Miskotte's remembrance was wrong, however, when he dates these initiatives back to the first year of the German Occupation. In the context of his PhD research on Jan Koopmans, Niels den Hertog discovered an announcement by Miskotte himself in the church journal that listed preachers for the next Sunday (*Het Amsterdams Predikbeurtenblad*).[6] In this announcement, dated to May 16, 1941, Miskotte promotes a course on "the basics (*grondlijnen*, ground-lines) of the biblical message," to be held in the New Church, the central medieval church at the Dam square; the goal of the course was to equip its attendees to lead Bible-reading groups afterward in neighborhoods all over the city. Miskotte explains:

> It should not become a series of apologetic lectures; thus, one does not have to expect edification or a defence of truth—it will simply be a matter of instruction. We will convene as a *beit-hammidrash*, a house of learning.

Of course, it is significant that Miskotte uses here a Jewish expression for a meeting that is not *in* the synagogue, but *alongside* the synagogue. It may well be that he had in mind the "Free Jewish Learning House" of Franz Rosenzweig and others in Frankfurt when he wrote this notice. At any rate, he did not intend for the meetings to be a church service, where Word and Sacrament were celebrated or confession and obedience presupposed. Rather, he meant for this course to host a common effort of learning *without* presuppositions—including the presupposition that it makes sense to read the Bible together because the Bible is a good, important, or foundational book. Soon after his announcement, Miskotte evidently provided a hall for this course in the New Church, and in summer 1941, he expanded his lessons into a booklet entitled *Biblical ABCs*, which was edited (in two editions) in the autumn by the usual publishing house of more popular materials by Dutch dialectical theologians: Callenbach in Nijkerk. The appearance of this manuscript in print implies that German authorities permitted its dissemination. Other books by Miskotte from the same period received a negative assessment from the National Socialist Movement in the Netherlands and its censors; one such work was *Messiaans Verlangen* (*Messianic Desire*), a study of the lyric of Henriëtte Roland Holst-Van der Schaik, a Dutch activist and poet, who can be compared to someone like Rosa Luxemburg.[7] But *Biblical ABCs* didn't sustain such a verdict—though one may wonder how the association of sanctification with *sabotage* (usually an act of a militant resistance! see chapter 10 section 1a) could pass the censor. Nonetheless: Miskotte clearly aimed in 1941 to offer the spiritual foundations for resistance, but in this text he didn't *openly* criticize the propaganda and the terrible measures of the Occupation force and its accomplices.

Another point of attention for reading the present work concerns the already-mentioned distinction that Miskotte makes between preaching and instruction, or, in the language of the Gospels, between *kērygma* and *didachē*. *Biblical ABCs* does *not* mean a short reproduction of the *content* of the Bible in order to adhere to its truth and convert to its appeal. This title means only, and in a strict sense: an acquaintance with the Bible's *language*, in expectation that this specific language will bring a specific message and a specific way of life to light. In this procedure, Miskotte's presuppositions are, firstly, that it makes sense to distinguish phenomenology (the art of observing) from theology (the art of decision-making), and secondly, that it doesn't belong to the range of human knowledge to discern what God is doing with the hearts and minds of those who read Scripture. As a result, Miskotte's concentration on biblical *language* leads to a predominant concentration on the language of the *Old Testament*, the Hebrew Bible. And as such, this concentration implicitly expresses solidarity with the Jewish people, who were extremely threatened in 1941. More than 100,000 members of the Jewish people from the Netherlands—probably some 60,000 of them from Amsterdam alone—would not, in the end, survive the Shoah.

So far I have described the main contributions of the book that now lies in your hand. In the Introduction that follows, I will sketch the factors in Miskotte's life and work that made him the right person to lay the foundations for resistance during *that* moment and in *this* way. I will also describe some aspects of the book's first reception and indicate the character of the additions that the author himself would make to the book in its postwar edition of 1966.

MISKOTTE'S VIGILANCE IN THE 1930S: A SKETCH OF FIVE STEPS TOWARD *BIBLICAL ABCS*

1. Miskotte, at that moment thirty-eight years old, defended his PhD thesis on December 17, 1932, at the University of Groningen, nearly two months before Hitler came to power in the Netherland's eastern neighbor. The subject of this, Miskotte's third attempt at a dissertation, was quite unusual. It dealt with Judaism, not in its classical Talmudic expression but as reflected in a range of its contemporary philosophical representatives. Its title, *Het wezen der joodse religie* (*The Essence of Jewish Religion*),[8] indicates the use of the phenomenological method of *Wesensschau*, the "intuition of essences." Instructed by Max Brod, Miskotte distinguished Judaism from paganism and Christianity as the three fundamental types of being human. (We will return to Miskotte's conception of *paganism* below.) Next, in an analysis of the thinking of Hermann Cohen, Martin Buber, and Franz Rosenzweig, Miskotte systematically sketched the characteristics of Judaism, with some attention also to extreme positions such as those of Franz Kafka (exceptional as a Jewish adherent of original sin) and Ernst Bloch (utopian and messianic). In Miskotte's eyes, the most important witness in this company was Franz Rosenzweig, whose *Star of Redemption* he had bought from the bookstand of the local Jewish congregation at the Pressa, an international press exhibition in Cologne in 1928. He read it intensively and assessed it as the writing of a great thinker and a great theologian, too. In a certain sense, Miskotte's dissertation is his most scholarly work, in that reconstructing the Jewish religion is more important than elaborating its possible contribution to Christian theology. Only the last chapters compare Jewish interpretations of the Hebrew Bible with a Christian reading of the Old Testament, specifically one shaped by the nineteenth-century Christian preacher H.F. Kohlbrugge.[9] Kohlbrugge had deeply influenced the spiritual atmosphere in Miskotte's parental house, especially the piety of his mother. In agreement with Hermann Cohen, Miskotte's dissertation describes Judaism as a religion of "correlation," where the Godhead makes itself dependent on the human covenant-partner, that is, on the moral action of the people of Israel. By contrast, for Kohlbrugge, sanctification always is and remains a divine gift, passively received by the human sinner. Therefore, for the Miskotte of 1932, there is a *dispute* between the Jewish and the Christian (or Reformation) reading of the same Scripture. This would remain his opinion, including in the *Biblical ABCs*, but through the dramatic developments of the following years, this aspect would gradually recede.

2. In March 1934, Miskotte wrote an article for the *Journal of the Christian Student Movement*. In it, he makes a point in a quite opposite direction. The title of the article is "Judaism as a Question to the Church."[10] If his dissertation raised this theme only implicitly, here it emerges directly: namely, what

it means for the church that it encounters Judaism as another post-Biblical religion besides itself. Miskotte argues that in the whole of its being, Judaism is *asking*, and thereby *challenging*, the church. It asks, at least tacitly: "Why are you, Christians, such a resting, reposing people? Where can we see your contestation with things as they are?" "Where is your earnest prayer for the coming of the Kingdom of Heaven?" "And when you are saying that the Messiah has already come, how can you show that you have actually come further, and that the expectations of the prophets have been fulfilled?" "If the promises were fulfilled in Jesus, why don't we see a redeemed reality in the world?" "Moreover, why do you pretend to have a missionary appointment towards *us*, whereas we cannot recognize in your message the direction of the Scriptures you received from us?" "And how can we determine that you actually are keeping the divine commandments?" Miskotte does not offer a Christian theological theory, either an old one or a new, to demonstrate his answers to these questions—or better: to this *one* question in its many variants. Instead, he encourages the church to persist in being disturbed by Judaism: by a Judaism that is a *questioning* of the church's whole existence, in its claim of being the people of the Messiah. In his diaries of the 1930s, which have now been mostly edited and published, we can study how Miskotte himself as a Christian preacher and theologian tried to let these questions penetrate his soul and his heart. This approach to Judaism as a fundamental question appears in the emphasis of *Biblical ABCs* on *expectation* as a keyword in biblical language. Such an emphasis also reveals the "pagan" character of bourgeois western culture in the eighteenth and nineteenth centuries, for which *expectation* is exactly *not* a keyword (chapter 11, sections 1–4).

3. A month later, in April 1934, another Miskotte article appeared, a chapter contribution for a volume in which some so-called dialectical theologians in the Netherlands introduced themselves. Miskotte's chapter is titled "Some Remarks on Theological Exegesis." It would later feature in German translation in the Festschrift for Karl Barth's fiftieth birthday in 1936, under the title "The Problem of Theological Exegesis."[11] This article is important for understanding Miskotte's whole theological development, because in it he lays out his view on the contribution of the phenomenological method to biblical exegesis; *Biblical ABCs* entirely presupposes this earlier work. Miskotte distinguishes three dimensions within the exegetical enterprise: to look—to see—to hear. *Looking* is the task of the modern historical-critical method: we have to carefully acknowledge the text in the contextual-historical conditions of its origins. *Hearing* is the task of faith, which obediently and attentively tries to learn and to do what God through God's Word is asking of us today. However, between looking and hearing there exists a tension: between a scientific and an ecclesial vantage, respectively. In both the past and in the present, the two tasks tend toward polarization and mutual incomprehension. According to Miskotte, such tension is inevitable, but polarization is

undesirable. The approach of the middle category, *seeing*, can offer room for a better encounter between the outer two approaches that are more extreme in character. *Seeing* designates the task of asking for meaning, but without the immediate need to transpose the acquired insight as to the meaning of the text into an existential decision on the part of the reading and interpreting subject. That is the implication of the Husserlian category of *epochē*, "suspension of judgment." One can acknowledge some "structures" in texts and in the cultural environment (or in the *Lebensgefühl*) by which texts express themselves—but without directly adhering to their implications for one's own life. Here we can recognize the method of the later *Biblical ABCs*, which stresses the *language* and the *grammar* of the biblical text while suspending the question of its truth. In comparison with his dissertation, a new element in this article on "theological exegesis" is its reference to the Bible translation by Buber and Rosenzweig, as well as to some lectures in which they explain and defend their translation procedure. Miskotte's dissertation presents these two Jewish witnesses only as systematic thinkers, but the article honors their contributions to exegesis. For example, Miskotte takes up from them an enriched understanding of *dabar*, Hebrew for "word" or "thing," as a correction of the usual Christian conviction about the Word. So, too, he finds inspiration in Rosenzweig for reconsidering the unity of the canon and the significance of the ordering of pericopes as well as the connections between texts through "lead words" (*Leitwörter*).

4. From 1932 onward, Miskotte's diaries very accurately follow developments in politics and in the churches of Germany. He was extremely anxious about the increasing antisemitism, and he held no illusions about the disgraceful methods of the Nazis toward their enemies. Given the profile of his mind, there is some cause for amazement about this. For from his youth onward, Miskotte possessed a deeply felt nature mysticism; he had a romantic disposition and a preference for dark and earthy German poetry. All those characteristics *might* have been made him sympathetic to the conservative revolution, especially in Germany. But apparently he escaped that danger and was saved from it—perhaps exactly by studying the prophetic voices of contemporary Judaism. In this way, he became one of the earliest, most sensible, and most vigilant figures in the cause of antifascism in the Netherlands.

The category within which Miskotte perceived the reactionary spirit of the 1930s was that of *paganism*, in the sense that Max Brod used the term.[12] It is important to understand how Miskotte distinguished *the Christian* as a third way of being human beside *the pagan* and *the Jew*. One faction in the Nazi Party of Germany sought a revival of "native" Germanic religion (of course in what we now call a "reinvented" way). If, in the Netherlands, some in the orbit of National Socialism saw in the old twelfth-century mythological-poetic Icelandic epic, the Edda, intimations of their own spirit, Miskotte determined to take the gesture seriously, not as a mere ideological invention. For a better understanding of this current, Miskotte read many books by reactionary thinkers, who argued that the Jewish spirit had tried to intoxicate the people of Europe, and that Christianity in a certain sense derived from this blameworthy Judaism. For Miskotte, Christians in Europe are pagans who have been disturbed (*gestoord*) by the proclamation of Israel's message in their context. As such, Miskotte's definition of a Christian is a disturbed pagan. It is, consequently, not just a rhetorical flourish but a true self-confession when Miskotte says: "we must *honor* paganism, because we have to acknowledge that we are pagans ourselves." And that insight explains Miskotte's great project of the late thirties: *Edda and Torah: A Comparison of Germanic and Israelite Religion*. That book appeared at the beginning of October 1939, when the double invasion of Poland had already begun World War II, though the Netherlands still strove (delusively) to maintain its neutrality.[13]

Some critics of Miskotte's project hold that in this approach he overestimated the religious component in the Nazi ideology. On the other hand, in our early twenty-first century, many extreme thinkers of the "conservative revolution" from that time—such as Ludwig Klages, Janko Janeff, Friedrich Hielscher, or Leopold Ziegler—are intensively studied and discussed on neo-Nazi websites; they are increasingly influential again, or still. In Miskotte's eyes, their appeal to pre-Christian Germanic religion could be confirmed by reading the *Edda*. This use of the so-called Edda, once published, elicited well-founded criticism on historical and philological grounds from the Germanist professor Jan de Vries, who personally sympathized with National Socialism.[14] However, the feelings and the attitude toward life of his fascist contemporaries, which Miskotte recognized in these old texts, show their own coherence: life is dominated by fate, the beginning of all things is chaos, and in the end, all gods and all humans go to ruin; in between, only *struggle* takes place, where the strongest are heroes and the weak are held in contempt. In considering Christianity, Miskotte did not consult a single basic text; given its character as paganism disturbed by Israel, Christendom represents a syncretistic entity, and is therefore unfit for such a comparison. Instead, Miskotte contrasts the Edda with the *Torah*: the latter is the witness of an encounter between a speaking God and a responding people. It testifies of a good Creation at the beginning and a completed Kingdom at the end, and since it aims at justice, it commends the person who protects weak people. In this way, Miskotte thought that standing up for the foundational text of Judaism was the best way to defend the values of humanity, and also in the end to defend the Christian Church under the threat of oppression. Miskotte was convinced that this threat would come, and that it would come *soon*.

5. A last element of the prehistory of *Biblical ABCs* occurred on Saturday, January 6, 1940. On that day Miskotte received in his letterbox Volume II.1 of Karl Barth's *Church Dogmatics*.[15] Miskotte had many objections to Barth's theology as he initially encountered it in the second *Letter to the Romans*. However, at the end of the 1920s, Barth personally helped him to overcome

some serious problems in his ministry, and Miskotte gradually grew in an admiration for "the Master," though never without some criticism. On that day at the beginning of 1940, Miskotte did as he usually did when one of Barth's volumes appeared, reading and studying it intensely in less than forty-eight hours (also preaching in between). *Horaion!* (Greek for "splendid!"), he wrote in his diary. Especially the doctrine of the divine "perfections" (traditionally: attributes) in this volume was of great importance for him. Later (in 1956) he would explain his enthusiasm in a contribution to the Festschrift for Barth's seventieth birthday (titled "Permission for a Scriptural Thinking"). There, Miskotte characterizes *CD* II.1 as the draft of "an *Israelite* doctrine of God," because of Barth's openness to the "theological depth exactly of the *primitive* language (about God in Scripture)." Methodologically, Miskotte praises what he calls "the induction out of the Name" instead of "the deduction out of a concept." For the method of *Biblical ABCs*, this insight is decisive. One doesn't have to start with a general concept of "God" and then afterward derive several divine attributes from this concept. Rather, one must start with the concrete Name of the God of Israel, which is at the same time known *and* unknown to us, and then afterward, one thinks through the implications of this reliable Name, who wants to communicate with us. Moreover, one need not start with general, metaphysical attributes and then afterward discern the virtues by which the Name is compassionate and just toward us. Instead the reasoning must proceed the other way around: from the Mercy and Justice of God to God's Power to be merciful and just. In my judgment, Miskotte tends to neglect Barth's appreciation for the tradition of scholasticism, and I would then say that methodologically, *CD* II.1 and *Biblical ABCs* are not following quite the same path. It seems indubitable to me, however, that reading Barth's volume gave decisive inspiration to Miskotte, and that his booklet of 1941 would not have yielded the same clarity and tendency without his encounter with *this* part of the *Church Dogmatics*.

MISKOTTE AND THE *BIBLICAL ABCS* DURING THE GERMAN OCCUPATION OF THE NETHERLANDS

Miskotte worried that he would be arrested and punished (by deportation to a camp?) because of having written *Edda and Torah* (diary entry from August 25, 1939). Also, his public debate with the reverend Lodewijk Ekering, member of the National Socialist Movement, at a special meeting of the council of the Amsterdam Reformed Church on February 27, 1939—after which meeting the church council refused to take a clear position (!)—could have made the German authorities suspicious of him. Later during the war, Miskotte willingly jeopardized himself and his family by illegally hiding Jewish people in his house. Furthermore, the activities of the resistance group the *Lunterse kring* continued; they instigated the Synod to more clearly protest shameless injustice, and they sent couriers to Switzerland (via Barth in Basel and via Visser 't Hooft in Geneva) to keep in contact with the Dutch government-in-exile in London. But apparently, none of these were grounds enough to arrest Miskotte. Although the Nazi censors immediately forbade his *Edda and Torah*, by May of 1940 nearly all copies had already sold out. The occupying forces prohibited only Miskotte's appointment to a professorship in Groningen, thereby menacing the theological faculty. There is no reason to regret that outcome, though, because the universities were soon closed, and the church appointed Miskotte to pursue Bible work amid an educated public in the southern quarters of Amsterdam. This special appointment gave him opportunity to develop the catechetical program that *Biblical ABCs* would expand: to equip people for a "better resistance" in favor of justice and humanity over against the advancing forces of death.

From April 1944 onward, Miskotte hid himself during the nights at other addresses than his own home, and so did his friend Koopmans. Together, both comrades could suddenly appear among their colleagues, to encourage the irresolute and to admonish the cowards. On March 12, 1945, the Germans shot twenty-four persons dead in reprisal for the gunning down of a member of their security force (*Sicherheitsdienst*) by the armed resistance. One of the bullets moved over the head of the victims and struck Koopmans, who was watching from behind the window of his hiding place. After twelve days he died because of his wounds. It was the same, much-mourned Koopmans who wrote the (in my perception) most impressive review of the *Biblical ABCs*, for the Amsterdam church journal of February 13, 1942.[16] He remembered another famous work in the history of Dutch theology: *Herschepping* (*Recreation*), a very original dogmatics for laypeople by Oepke Noordmans, written in 1934. "That book," Koopmans said,

> was an outcome of the First World War. It tried to understand the doctrine of the Church in a new way. But meanwhile, seven years later, a storm rages over Europe. And now we have been thrown back to the most elementary datum, i.e., to the reading of the Bible itself, and therewith to the question of how the structure of learning has to be in a biblical sense.

Koopmans closes his review of *Biblical ABCs* with these words:

> Through this war, God teaches us to ask for the Bible. In the meanwhile, the basics of our existence have become considerably narrower. We almost don't have a Church anymore, apart from the form in which it can be found in the Bible. And perhaps we must release what we do have that is more than that. In that situation, it is of great importance to have been instructed how to read the Bible.

Personally, I'm deeply impressed by these words, and I wonder whether many of the problems we deal with nowadays in theology will fade away in the perspective of an urgency such as Koopmans expressed.

THE POSTWAR EDITION OF 1966

After World War II, the effort to reconstruct the country generally suppressed attention to the spiritual struggles that took place during the war. In the Netherlands, it was not until the 1960s that a revival of interest in the years of the German Occupation would begin.

After his retirement in December 1959, Miskotte began to work on a new edition of his former publications. All the titles mentioned in this Introduction received a reedition, and often at the same time a revision also. In the case of *Biblical ABCs*, Miskotte remembered that in the Foreword of the 1941 edition, he had expressed his wish to write a deeper and broader study in better times. In 1966, he determined that this study had already appeared. It was *When the Gods are Silent: On the Meaning of the Old Testament* (Dutch 1956; German translation 1963; English translation 1967).[17] For him, the publication of this work made the task of rewriting the *ABCs* easier. Besides the addition of poems, hymns, and stanzas from the new Dutch rhymed version of the Genevan Psalms, and some larger excurses on biblical language (i.e., what is the biblical word for *liberation*? What does *the day of YHWH* mean?), I will distinguish two categories of major additions.

First, in 1966 it was possible to be more explicit about the circumstances of oppression and resistance that marked the book in its first edition. Miskotte could now more openly express the deep connection between the readers of this book and the people of Israel. He could mention the initial intuition that reading the Bible could help to resist the menace of the Third Reich; and he could refer to the SS, the Confessing Church, and so on.

Secondly, Miskotte now alluded to the typical debates of the 1960s. In this way, (a) he discusses the anti-authoritarian atmosphere of those days—remarking that the Dutch word that indicates authority (*gezag*) is related to the word for "saying" (*zeggen, het gezegde*), and, in good Reformation fashion, that precisely the Word that God speaking to me generates my liberation and my "coming of age" (*Mündigkeit*; chapter 1). Furthermore, (b) he hints at the newly revived discussion of the "death of God," and hence discusses atheism in a more extensive way (chapter 5). He also (c) comes back to the struggling that humans do in the Bible concerning God and God's relationship to evil (chapter 6), a question that had always engaged Miskotte, but which had been postponed in the heat of the struggle for justice and liberation. Miskotte then reacts to the assertion that the young generation of the 1960s should be "a skeptical generation" (chapter 12), but he argues that this generation in its optimism to improve the world isn't skeptical *enough*. And finally, on the last page of the book, he responds to the new movements in literary criticism to regard the Bible as literature. This assertion is not incorrect, Miskotte says, but at the same time it is *easier*: for the sense of humanity that the Bible communicates is not a literary motif, but a deep feeling; a feeling of *simplicity* arising from the particularity of the Name, and at the same time, with a universal tendency.

I conclude that the translators of this book did not deprive its English-speaking readers of essential insights by their decision to omit these additions from 1966, striving as they have to preserve the atmosphere of the historical circumstances under which the book of 1941 was written.

NOTES

1. Rudolph P. Cleveringa, "Rede naar aanleiding van het ontslag van prof. Mr. E.M. Meijers, uitgesproken op 26 november 1940, als Decaan van de Juridische Faculteit," published during the occupation by some underground journals and after the war in *Leids Universiteits Blad* 11 (1945): 5–13.

2. Jan Koopmans, *Bijna te laat!*, published after the war in *Het verzet der Hervormde Kerk*, ed. H.C. Touw, 2 vols. (Gravenhage: Boekencentrum, 1946), 2:209–216.

3. This group, with origins in the Dutch Protestant circles that contacted the German Confessing Church, included members of the Gereformeerde Kerken in Hersteld Verband (Reformed Churches in Restored Union). See Ger van Roon, *Protestants Nederland en Duitsland 1933–1941* (Utrecht/Antwerpen: Het Spectrum, 1973).

4. K.H. Miskotte, "Betere weerstand," in *Het verzet der Hervormde Kerk*, 2:222–227. Now also in K.H. Miskotte, *Messiaans verlangen en andere literatuur en cultuurkritische opstellen,* Verzameld Werk Vol. 12 (Kampen: Kok, 1999), 462–468.

5. Karl Barth, "Eine Frage und eine Bitte an die Protestanten von Frankreich," in idem, *Eine Schweizer Stimme 1938–1945* (Zürich: EVZ, 1945), 147–156; now also in idem, *Offene Briefe 1935–1942*, ed. Diether Koch, Karl Barth Gesamtausgabe Abt. V, Briefe (Zürich: TVZ, 2001), 238–251, here 250: "der Geist des christlichen Ansatzes zu neuem, besseren Widerstand." English translation: "The Church and the War: A Letter by Professor Karl Barth to a French Pastor," *Theology* 237 (1940): 209–217.

6. Cf. Willem van der Meiden, "*Bijbels ABC*, een polemische grammatica," *In de Waagschaal* 46 (2017): 1, 7–10.

7. K.H. Miskotte, *Messiaansch verlangen: Het lyrisch werk van Henriëtte Roland Holst* (Amsterdam: Uitgeverij Holland, 1941), now in idem, *Messiaans Verlangen*, 13–194.

8. K.H. Miskotte, *Het Wezen der Joodsche Religie* (Amsterdam: Paris, 1933); third edition in idem, Verzameld Werk Vol. 6 (Kampen: Kok, 1982). German translation: *Das Wesen der jüdischen Religion*, trans. Heinrich Braunschweiger (Berlin: LIT Verlag, 2017).

9. Cf. H.F. Kohlbrugge, *Wozu das Alte Testament? Anleitung zur richtigen Schätsung der Bücher Mosis und der Propheten* (Elberfeld: Verlag der Niederländischen reformierten Gemeinde, 1855).

10. K.H. Miskotte, "Het jodendom als vraag aan de kerk," *Eltheto* 88 (1933/34): 6. Now in idem, *Theologische opstellen,* Verzameld Werk Vol. 9 (Kampen: Kok, 1990), 89–97.

11. K.H. Miskotte, "Opmerkingen over theologische exegese," in *De openbaring der verborgenheid*, ed. M.C. Slotemaker de Bruïne (Baarn: Bosch & Keuning, 1934), 63–99; German: "Das Problem der theologischen Exegese," in *Theologische Aufsätze: Karl Barth zum 50. Geburtstag*, ed. Ernst Wolf (München: Chr. Kaiser, 1936), 51–77. A critical edition will be published in Miskotte's Verzameld Werk Vol. 16 (forthcoming).

12. Max Brod, *Heidentum, Christentum, Judentum: ein Bekenntnisbuch*, 2 vols. (München: Kurt Wolff Verlag, 1921).

13. K.H. Miskotte, *Edda en Thora: een vergelijking van Germaanse en Israëlitische religie* (Nijkerk: C.F. Callenbach, 1939). Now in idem, Verzameld Werk Vol. 7 (Kampen: Kok, 1983). German translation: *Edda und Thora: ein Vergleich germanischer und israelischer Religion*, trans. Heinrich Braunschweiger (Berlin: LIT Verlag, 2015).

14. Jan de Vries, "Boekbeoordelingen: K.H. Miskotte, *Edda en Thora*," *Nieuw Theologisch Tijdschrift* 29 (1940): 151–157, republished in *"Wij willen het heidendom eeren": Miskotte en de "nieuwe tijd*," ed. Chris Doude van Troostwijk et al. (Baarn: Ten Have, 1994), 243–249.

15. K.H. Miskotte, *Uit de dagboeken 1938–1940*, Verzameld Werk Vol. 5c (Utrecht: Kok, 2018), 855. On Miskotte's estimation of *Church Dogmatics* II.1, see his "Die Erlaubnis zum schriftgemäßem Denken," in *Antwort: Festschrift zum 70 Geburtstag von Karl Barth*, ed. Eduard Thurneysen (Zürich: EVZ, 1956), 29–51; now also in Miskotte, *Karl Barth: Inspiratie en vertolking: Inleidingen, essays, briefwisseling,* Verzameld Werk Vol. 2 (Kampen: Kok 1987), 196–220.

16. Jan Koopmans, "Boekbespreking K.H. Miskotte, *Bijbelsch ABC*," *Kerkbeurtenblad voor Amsterdam en omgeving* 16 (1942): 20.

17. K.H. Miskotte, *Als de goden zwijgen: Over de zin van het Oude Testament* (Amsterdam: uitgeversmaatschappiij Holland, 1956); 4th edition in: Verzameld Werk Vol. 9 (Kampen: Kok, 1983); German translation: *Wenn die Götter schweigen: vom Sinn des Alten Testaments*, trans. Heinrich Stoevesandt (München: Chr. Kaiser Verlag, 1966); English translation: *When the Gods are Silent*.

Chapter 1

Reading Scripture

One characteristic of the change of epochs we are living through is a new attentiveness to the biblical witness. Among Reformed, Roman Catholic, and liberal Christians alike, we find a more intense concentration on interpreting the Bible than has been the case in—dare we say it—centuries. One hears talk everywhere about the bond between Europe and Scripture, and about the biblical ideas that undergird the rule of law. In the dark winter of 1940 we saw how both churched and unchurched people gathered themselves around the light and the shadow cast from the open book. Dozens of Bible studies were founded in the major cities. These were neither pietistic small groups nor debating societies; most of the time they weren't study clubs, either. What exactly they were and what they meant to their participants is hard to say, because it concerns the mystery of the church itself. And the mystery of the church is, that something happens there.

THE WORD HAPPENS.

This innermost mystery is surrounded by a wide zone of reflecting and seeking and drawing near. Apart from the Word that strikes, there is the work of engaging with Scripture as the witness to that Word: as a sphere of wisdom, as tutor and guide, as help and support, as lift and propulsion. In other words, a zone where the Bible is not waived off as a merely formal authority, or treated as an arsenal for argument, or a green pasture for troubled minds, dredging up prooftexts and pious slogans from a confused whole, but where

SCRIPTURE IS OPENED AS A WORLD

to dwell in, to live out of, to be truly hidden in and truly armed by.

The guilt of the church—alas, every reason exists (and new reasons, too) to expound it! The church neglects its call to mission, it practices social responsibility half-heartedly, it deeply lacks community and a willingness to sacrifice. It has become bourgeois; it has slackened and grown complacent and willfully ignorant about the actual powers that rule the world and humankind. It is blind to the gods of our time that we say do not possess us when they possess us to the bone! But the real guilt and real need lie elsewhere. The church has not acknowledged *any* authority for itself, and it has not proclaimed any authority in the world. By limiting God's authority and diverting Christ's influence, the church confines the Spirit's work to the "inner life"—and all of this amounts to a courteous denial. It effectively undermines the truth by which the church stands or falls.

When, then, there is a first stirring of new life—an awakening, a rubbing of the eyes, a fumbling for footing, a joyful recognition of the half-seen and half-confessed; when now a fear arises and a questioning whether judgment can still be averted—if those first signs of life are now expanding in all directions, bringing strangers together, and new resolutions pierce indolence, then such movement emerges from nothing else than the apprehension; the premonition of

THE PRESENCE OF TRUTH.

"See, among you stands one whom you do not know" (John 1:26). The real disgrace of this "not-knowing" is nevertheless *surpassed* in luminosity by the dawning realization:

> Surely, this commandment that I am commanding you today is not too hard for you, nor is it too far away. It is not in heaven, that you should say, "Who will go up to heaven for us, and get it for us so that we may hear it and observe it?" Neither is it beyond the sea, that you should say, "Who will cross to the other side of the sea for us, and get it for us so that we may hear it and observe it?" No, the Word is very near to you; it is in your mouth and in your heart for you to observe. See, I have set before you today life and prosperity, death and adversity (Deut 30:11–15).

This apprehension—this realization had been considered as fact among broad swathes of our public.

BUT NOW THE DANGER!

—the danger, that is, that we would allow the whole subject to devolve into pietism; that we would revert to atavistic spiritual-mindedness; that the phantom of previous generations might return to haunt the byways of this budding new life, and we would become, like them, Bible-believing—but not Bible-compliant as we ought to be. Or even worse: we would learn anew to discuss and dispute without undergoing baptism—that is, submersion into the presence of truth, irreducible truth. As God's truth, it stands grounded on nothing but itself. It asserts and commends itself. It justifies and exalts itself! The danger is that we would talk and talk and believe our own talking, our own rightness and would-be rightness before we have seen, individually and together, that

AUTHORITY PRECEDES.

Should we fail to heed the danger, it would mean that we, lonely children of earth, are left again to our loneliness. We would then be responsible to raise ourselves instead of being raised; to forge our own path through the thicket of opinions instead of being transferred into the world and indeed the Kingdom of the "Father of the spirits of all flesh" (Num 16:22, 27:17; Heb 12:9).

Self-education is no education. We cannot come to Scripture; we must proceed from it. There can be fruitful movement in all directions within the good life, but only when we choose our position: or rather, when we are chosen to take our place at the heart of this truth and reality. It is a hundred times easier to rationalize the authority of Scripture than the authority of the totalitarian state or some pagan worldview. But this must not take place, because, in the final analysis, it cannot. God's Word would not be *God's* Word if it were possible to ground its authority in something outside of itself. Authority precedes! But now, formulated positively, what is needed? What will curb our tendency to justify ourselves using the Bible? What will divest us from our sectarian strivings?

How do we find true freedom *proceeding from* authority?

What factors hinder us, that we misunderstand this authority? Authority is here identical to *that which is authored*, insofar as this presents itself to us in its own aspect. It is not forced upon us, but offered to us. It sheds light and draws us to the light. It occupies us, far more than a work of art or a speech. It doesn't win our heart over through subjugation but through emancipation. Scripture does not rob us of autonomy, but initiates us into a more intense originality. The Word comes to us with a simplicity that puts our complications to shame. Given this experience, what then of all this dispute and hairsplitting, all this rationalization and gnat-straining, sniping and grousing, parties and cliques, forerunners and rearguards?

Much could be said about this topic from the perspective of psychology and sociology. If anything could hinder or heal this overcomplication, it is understanding the *spiritual grammar* of Scripture.

THE UNDERSTANDING

Namely, the understanding of what we read, insofar as we submit to its grip. For authority to yield sustainable guidance, we must constantly hear it and take this question seriously: "Do you understand what you read?" (Acts 8:30). We do not ask the question preemptively, so as to test whether we would accept authority. Rather, we ask from after the fact, dependent on the content of Scripture. We must learn to understand from the presence of truth. To notice differences, to draw borders; to trace the forms and contours and to receive their imprint, we must let the *grondlijnen* or ground-lines, the *grondwoorden* or ground-words, the spiritual grammar of Scripture instruct us. This is the rationale for all contemporary institutions such as Bible studies, to which all other churchly initiatives should be subordinate. Understanding the fundamental matter at hand! But understanding the subject matter will be impossible without understanding the particular language within which the subject is embedded. Reading is a crucial function.

READING IS LEARNING

The point is so elementary as to embarrass us, yet we soon discover that it remains largely unfamiliar and untested. We have not yet lived and worked with it. What we have lost sight of is this: the entirety of Scripture is anti-pagan testimony, while paganism is the natural religion of humankind. It takes a thousand forms but reflects a single intention.

We traipsed from one hallowed hall to another in the ivory tower of spiritual life, and we surpassed each other in lofty and profound and delicate wisdom, teaching, and principle—and yet we skipped elementary school, yes, even kindergarten. Now we understand why we were often afflicted with the feeling, that although we understood everything, we didn't actually grasp the principle subject. Though we admired it, we didn't dwell in its beauty; we were convinced of the truth, but we sought somewhere in a little corner of our heart to find support for ourselves in order that we might prop up the truth. Therefore:

BACK TO THE ABCs

—to the simple *grondlijnen*, ground-lines, of Holy Scripture and the living from out of it!

Simplicity is subject to a very curious misunderstanding. Those who are called simple are often farthest removed from the simplicity of Scripture. The latter's simplicity is the simplicity of eyes that see the unity, the one meaning, the single saving purpose of God.

The truly simple receive and learn wisdom, and then it becomes clear that they live very close to each other, even in their apparent contradictory intentions.

The meaning of the movement in our country to "activate" congregations spiritually through Bible study lies in the divinely willed turn to

THE SIMPLICITY
THE UNITY
THE HARMONY

More simplicity is needed; but it cannot be forced by storming into action.
More unity is needed; but it cannot be reached by camouflaging differences.
More harmony is needed; but it cannot exist without true simplicity and true unity.

This is why we need to understand *each other*; but in order to understand each other, we should *first* understand *Scripture together*: it is *the grondbestek* or ground design, the constitution, the model, the frame, the pattern, the fabric and its warp and weft. We read together; we learn together; and above all, just insofar as we do these things, we live together. From this center and centripetally, we work together to build togetherness in our society also, if this should be granted us.

Someone will say that this is a very long-term project indeed: to understand Scripture together! It has occupied many centuries, and the people that have lent themselves to the task have not become more united. But this is not true, strictly speaking: what unites us as Christians is much more than what divides us. Today we are experiencing this again.

I want to press this point even further: we are experiencing again how much we are connected with Israel through the holy Instruction that we have received from God.

But I will add: it would not be the first time that need drove the spirit of an entire people at breakneck speed, including the church in its totality—need, that is, to grasp the essence; to seek heartfelt engagement with the Message and the Teaching. The same phenomenon occurred in the early Reformation—about which we can never marvel enough. Where did it all come from? The enthusiasm, the personal certainty, the communal joy and the courage of martyrs? Nobody has fathomed this "historically." I think we can say about the uncounted multitude of both learned and unlearned people what Karl Barth says in his "Lutherfeier" (1933): "Luther was *simple* . . . exactly at the critical moment of his life (and also of the church's life, and of world history) . . . simple as a child reciting a little ditty learned by heart and who in that moment knows nothing else but that little ditty."[1]

Many cry out for *action*. But it could be, that the primordial action is *hearing*—the hearing that arose in former times as resistance against the worldly powers, giving rise to martyrdom and a new song; a new diaconate, a new confession, and suffering and action arose. And now: even though the ABCs are not in themselves the *essence*, they are the grammar necessary to avoid misunderstanding the essence. Such error would demolish even the soundest hope for taking action.

We cannot draw up blueprints for the highest things. Willingness is everything!

Making many books is a weariness of the flesh (Eccl 12:12). Learning from the *one* book, however: that is all-decisive.

It is time—high time—to take this earnestly, so that we may be able to withstand in the evil day, and "having done everything, to stand firm" (Eph 6:13b).

NOTE

1. Karl Barth, "Lutherfeier 1933," *Theologische Existenz heute* 4 (München: Chr. Kaiser Verlag, 1933).

Chapter 2

Teaching

1.

The word "teaching" occurs much more often in Scripture than we might think at first. To start with, the Hebrew word for teaching—*Torah*—lies beneath every instance of the word "law" in the Dutch *Statenvertaling*.[1] But this rendering is bound to cause misunderstanding, since most of us at any rate associate "law" with jurisprudence, regulations, the judiciary, and law enforcement.

Torah means Teaching: holy (i.e., special, consecrated, divine) *Instruction*. Certainly the law also belongs to this instruction, but then so does everything else contained in Scripture! The project as a whole nonetheless is and remains divine education, guidance, discipline, rebuke, and teaching. A living voice that takes no rest, a wakeful eye that neither slumbers nor sleeps. "I will instruct you, I will counsel you with my eye upon you" (Ps 32:8).

Notice Psalm 119, a long, apparently monotonous hymn on the Teaching. This psalm shows several synonyms and variants: testimony, decree, precept, way, word, faithful speech (v. 43), guidance, *Weisung*, reason (v. 11). But "Torah" remains the key and comprehensive idea; the synonyms and variants only give it further explanation and application. This Teaching is praised, sung, cherished, practiced, and expounded. It is a lamp to our feet and a light to our path (v. 105). It is our companion and our enjoyment; our encouragement in loneliness and alienation, in wildernesses and chaos and dark places.

2.

"Teaching" in this biblical sense should be understood as *neither pagan nor Jewish*. Paganism is the natural religion of human hearts. As such it produces not just myth and cult but also, in its later stages, *teaching*. But this teaching always and only consists in explanations of the world: as elucidation of cosmic enigmas. Judaism considers teaching in its aspect as moral admonition: as the implementation and ramifying of a legal system for a sacred people.

Torah is wider, warmer, and more personal. It lies in the hand of the One who has things to put right with a people, and who engages them unspeakably searchingly and unfathomably intimately.

INSTRUCTION

Instruction from God: a word about the Word, which *happened*—this is the heart of the matter. For in this instruction God is leading us on the way: the "way everlasting," which is to say, the way from everlasting to everlasting. This way stands firm and sure through all boundaries of the world. It is a new and living way, upon which even those who are blind by nature will not get lost.

3.

The *five books of Moses* are considered to be Torah, in the strict sense. They collect stories of primordial times, histories of ancestors, songs, laws, cultic protocol, and genealogy. All these materials together count as teaching, and indeed, as holy instruction—even though they lack the form of instruction, since they are without introduction or method or any of our usual pedagogical features. That which instructs inheres in the whole, which contains a diversity of forms. This holds true for Scripture in all its contours. The New Testament summarizes the Old Testament as "the Law and the Prophets"; the third canonical division, the Writings, is not usually mentioned, but it is meant as well. Sometimes the entire Old Testament in its three collections is designated by shorthand as Law, and thus as *Teaching*. So, for example, John 10:34: "Is it not written in your Law, 'I said, you are gods'?" (a citation from Psalm 82, which is in no way a book of Moses!).

4.

The New Testament presents a similar relation between its various contents and a convergent meaning, if we pay attention to the various meanings of the word "gospel." *Gospel* means, first, the *message*. Second, it means the *story* about the words, works, and miracles of the Messiah, Jesus, his self-witness and his suffering and death. Third, it means the *literary form*. Through the literary form we encounter the story, and through the story, the message. The literary form serves the story, and the story serves the message. This view is perspectival, moving from one to the other. In the gospel narrative itself, proverbs, parables, rebukes, and invitations stand next to one another. Thus it is written, and therefore also, spoken; thus too, is the message. Reading becomes seeing, and seeing becomes hearing. And hearing becomes doing what must be done, enduring what is given to endure. The story is teaching: such forms as proverb, parable, command, and counsel are subservient to it.

5.

The Teaching is a *triumph* over the darkness of life. Certainly a kind of radiance lies over, say, the epic; it shines, for example, over the epic poetry of Homer. Its luster originates in a defiance of death. But the Teaching presupposes death, death in a thousand different forms. In such a world, the teacher, the rabbi, stands ready to declare life: the year of the Lord's favor, the acceptable year (Luke 4:19). The true rabbi is elevated to a prophet, and the prophet is elevated to a priest, and the priest, to a king. Yet the Instruction already contains these offices. "And he taught them." "And he spoke the word to them" (Mark 2:2). "The word of the Lord grew mightily and prevailed" (Acts 19:20).

Where the teacher is, there the disciples should be also; and they do indeed come. Where instruction takes place, there learning should, too—and not just learning that comes in the usual curricular garb, but "everything that proceeds from God's mouth" (Matt 4:4); and not only what pleases us, but also what hinders us. "For whoever finds me finds life . . . all who hate me love death" (Prov 8:35, 36b).

6.

To learn is a *wholesome duty*. We cannot rear ourselves; nor are we well served by a caretaker who makes our work so agreeable that we no longer feel its force and pressure from without. Rather, we must learn; we must extend ourselves. We are neither in paradise nor in heaven. Learning always presupposes discipline and order. We must come to learn through

EXPERIENCE.

It is vexing that we must listen, and accept guidance, and allow ourselves to receive the imprint of learning, as prophets and apostles and the spiritual father in the book of Proverbs all commend ("my son . . . accept my discipline and become wise; my son, give me your heart," etc.)—this duty belongs to our position as Adam's children and as those called by God. No matter how officially a church renders instruction, this instruction remains basically unchurched insofar as the church lacks courage to proceed from this authority: to lay claim, that is, to the opportunity that all people can find something to learn here. "We know little, too little, Lord," is a complaint that should be answered with a word of thanksgiving: We have so much to learn! And there is much to take in:

> All scripture is inspired by God and is useful for teaching, for reproof, for correction, and for training in righteousness (or: right relationship with God), so that everyone who belongs to God (the person who stands in this right relationship) may be proficient, equipped for every good work (2 Tim 3:16–17).

7.

Teaching is instruction from God that unifies these three elements: (a) *what is right* (b) *right judgment* (c) *the right direction, pointed out to us*. Truth is not just for contemplation; it separates and it forces decisions, either to the left or right. Truth is the reality of God meeting our spirit; it manifests as a presence that comes and renders judgment on the condition of our lonely, bewildered spirit—a judgment that harms and nullifies. In the final analysis, truth is guidance into a wide and open and yet still quite definite life. The Teaching points to the room, but the room does not contain absolute, empty possibility. Rather, it is a room of definite and fulfilled possibility. "I have seen a limit to all perfection, but your commandment is exceedingly broad" (Ps 119:96).

The Teaching is broad and complete in these three aspects:

What is RIGHT
Right JUDGMENT
Right DIRECTION

7a.

It follows that the human who experiences the address of truth must be ready to answer: to improve and to change. The majority of church people do not want to submit themselves to this authority, and their resistance presents a continual burden that presses especially heavy on Protestantism. The better way—or at least what one clearly suspects is better—is not accepted because it comes "from without"; because it is "imposed on us." We should grow more alert to the denial of all spiritual authority, which is an anarchy within the heart of good citizens. Where this attitude is rampant or gains respect, no biblical instruction is possible. Truly learning means to learn obedience from those who are positioned above oneself. Truly teaching requires that the teacher seek no higher gift than to be able themselves to learn. If we humans, and especially modern humans, must refute something, it is instruction that does *not* come with authority; instruction that does *not* come from outside us. What we must refute is instruction that flatters us with the idea that we stand on our own two feet and can see with our own eyes, without any aid. Such teaching is flippant and ungodly. It functions like a ladder that, after we have used it to climb up, we can then throw away in order to save ourselves and so to become "autonomous" (posing our own law upon ourselves).

8.

Instruction takes place under the saving power of the One who alone knows what is right, who alone has the right to render judgment, and who alone is able to give right direction to our lives.

All other instruction is, considered broadly, technical in nature, even philosophy. Other instruction is necessary as "first aid in case of emergency"—and as such remains provisional. It is as important as professional competency—and in the same way, it is unable to sustain us through fertile and barren years, in years of prosperity and adversity, under the rule of law and under the rule of power, in living and dying, in freedom and under the tyranny of godless people. The Teaching sustains us through constant guidance; its care never falters and its wisdom never fails. The Teaching accompanies us through the depths and over the plateaus. The Teaching destroys our loneliness. It sends us into the broad life.

9.

Take note of Ps 19:8–10a:

> the precepts of the Lord are right,
>   rejoicing the heart;
> the commandment of the Lord is clear,
>   enlightening the eyes;
> the fear of the Lord is pure,

> enduring for ever;
> the ordinances of the Lord are true
> > and righteous altogether.
> More to be desired are they than gold,
> > even much fine gold;
> sweeter also than honey,
> > and drippings of the honeycomb.

It now comes down to this, that we perceive that

ALL OF THE BIBLE IS TEACHING.

The books of Moses are as a whole called "teaching": with the result that the story of Abraham's sacrifice is teaching, and the genealogical register in Genesis 5 is teaching, and the unwilling testimony of Balaam is teaching. In the same way, it can be said of Scripture as a whole, the Old and the New Testaments together, that it is teaching in this rich, spiritual, and life-giving meaning that we have discovered. We can learn from anywhere within this teaching: we can learn *life*—what life is and what awakens life and how we need to live. Such learning is not one-time only, as if we know it for good. No, we approach this teaching time and time again. The God-fearing person meditates on Torah day and night (Ps 1:2).

Proclamation; claim; the community-constituting address of God to the children of men—all of these *arise* from Scripture. This is more than teaching! It is instead a momentary wonder: the event of the eternal Word in its coming. But Scripture, as it presents itself, is teaching. As such, Scripture is complete in itself and contains instruction concerning our reality and the One with whom we have to do. As the synagogue stood next to the temple in Israel, and next to the synagogue the *beit midrash*, the house of study, so also do Word and Sacrament stand next to catechesis. In a certain sense these holy mysteries presuppose a people that has already learned—and which continues to learn.

11.

Teaching is what we need, and this teaching is offered to us. *It is truly insane to think that catechesis should end with confirmation.* The sneering question of the liberal spirit is this: what is the real difference between teaching (*leer* in Dutch) and leather (also *leer* in Dutch)? The similarity is easier to indicate than the difference: both are needed to stand firmly in your shoes!

The sentence, "and they continued steadfastly in the apostles' doctrine" (Acts 2:42a), does not mean that they clung to a static truth, but that they continued to receive instruction from the living voice of the apostles. Their posture could not result in scholasticism then, and nor can it now. It leads instead to an increase in the knowledge of God, the living God. Life keeps moving; the Teaching keeps moving. We are never abandoned. There is always quiet communion; God personally governs us through Word and Spirit. No end is in sight.

12.

The church as God's servant on earth is at once *the subject* and *the object* of this instruction: it teaches and it learns. Sometimes it happens that one person imparts teaching and another person receives teaching, whether in a more formal or a more personal capacity. More basically, however, the church as such offers teaching as one who hears teaching, and insofar as the church hears, it allows others to hear with it. In that this teaching liberates, it also always binds.

As individuals, we are not left alone—but *neither* as a community. This would be the case if we equated the church with the Kingdom of God, and ecclesial authority with divine authority. But no! The church remains a disciple, even though it is endowed with the apostolate. Even now the church is not left to its own wisdom. We are not left alone with everything we have inherited, defenseless in the face of new questions that are hurled against us. We need not infer answers independently from what we have inherited. The Teaching *remains*, not only as a deposit, but also as a guide. There is thus every good reason for us, in likeness to the synagogue's feast of *Simchat Torah*,[2] to experience and to celebrate the

JOY OF TEACHING.

The goal of our learning and teaching is steadfast joy. God is good, therefore God instructs sinners in the way; God leads the humble in what is right, and teaches the humble God's way (Ps 25:8b, 9).

> He sends out his command to the earth;
>   his word runs swiftly . . .
> he makes his wind blow, and the waters flow.
> He declares his word to Jacob,
>   his statutes and ordinances to Israel.
> He has not dealt thus with any other nation;

they do not know his ordinances.
Praise the Lord! (Ps 147:16, 18–20)

For everything created by God is good, and nothing is to be rejected, provided it is received with thanksgiving; for it is sanctified by God's word and by prayer. If you put these instructions before the brothers and sisters, you will be a good servant of Christ Jesus, nourished on the words of the faith and of the sound teaching that you have followed. Have nothing to do with profane myths and old wives' tales. Train yourself in godliness (1 Tim 4:4–7).

Have nothing to do with stupid and senseless controversies; you know that they breed quarrel (2 Tim 2:23).

Pay close attention to yourself and to your teaching; continue in these things, for in doing this you will save both yourself and your hearers (1 Tim 4:16).

This means that the Teaching—which is Scripture, at least considered from the perspective of the instruction that arises from it—is also the fortress and protective wall of the *community*, protecting the simplicity, unity, and single-mindedness of those who are learning. On such grounds, several further things may be said about the Teaching. It is *not*

Self sufficient (i.e., requiring only one self)
One-sided
One-toned.

One can assert these things without posing the question of truth. Whether we believe the instruction or not, it presents itself to us in this way and claims this divine nature. Scripture lies before us like so, and in this respect cannot be misunderstood.

The teaching of the Torah is not self-sufficient (involving *one self*) in this sense: the Teaching never forms a world that is true or beautiful in and of itself. The world that Torah renders instead holds the capacity to germinate and to sustain *all good works*—works that may truly be called good because they honor God, follow God's commandment, and emerge from true faith; they "are not based on our own opinion or on precepts of men" (Heidelberg Catechism, Question 91).

The teaching is not *one-sided* in that it assumes no fixed form. Whatever form the teaching takes is in *service* to truth, and to *our* understanding of truth. The teaching does not cling to certain words but uses them to point to the riches of God's glory. Human contradictions do not hijack the teaching; it does not found a party but gathers a people, and that people is the new humanity.

The teaching is not *one-toned*: the unity by virtue of which the teaching subsists as *the* teaching, and through which it can be recognized and distinguished from other teachings, does not depend on repetition. The unity of the teaching lies rather in the striving together and mingling of *many voices*. Like a symphony, the teaching consists of many parts but one performance; or like an orchestra, with many instruments playing one musical piece.

What gives Scripture the power to *guide* people's spirits? In the first instance, Scripture bypasses the problems that *we* devise to directly counter our unconfessed need and alienation from God. Scripture instead speaks emphatically—maybe even self-sufficiently, one-sidedly, and mono-tonally—about this radical truth: *God is!* This dizzying fact not only casts life in a different light, but it *changes* our direction. In light of this particular uniqueness, one-sidedness and mono-tonality, our problems turn out to be quite bland and vain. The Teaching takes up the word: and it is rich, fertile, and multicolored, surpassing our imagination and expectation.

OUTLOOK

All of this has acquired a forceful accent at this time.

1

Concerning the World

a Many intellectual securities are demolished completely.
b An anti-intellectual teaching arises from instinct—from the blood.
c There is danger that empty lives, bitter hearts, and minds sick with doubt will bow before this teaching.

2

Concerning the Church

a Confessionalism—considered as a kind of clinging to the historic confessions—offers no satisfaction in this battle of spirits; what is required is an act of confession that joins head, heart, and hands. Confession can only be understood as the sediment of this act, which must be repeated and renewed.
b To "activate" the congregation does not heal its stultification, alienation from life, or bourgeoisification, so long as we don't know what the

church really *is*, where its salvation lies, and what its first vocation is: to learn and to live from out of the holy Teaching.

c All activity and endeavor of the congregation should proceed from and should be supported by a new biblical knowledge—of the ABCs.

3

A simple division of labor proves more difficult considering:

a The church is full of worldly inability to believe and unwillingness to learn.
b The world is full of homesickness for faith and willingness to learn.
c Modern nationalization appears to proclaim a totalitarian teaching of *salvation* proclaimed by worldly authority.
d The awakened church remembers under this pressure and threat that no teaching has total claim over all of life—except divine instruction in Scripture.

NOTES

1. This is the translation of the Bible into Dutch ordered by the Synod of Dordrecht in 1618 and financed by the Protestant Dutch Republic. Its stature compares to the King James Version in the Anglophone world.

2. *Simchat Torah* (Hebrew for "Joy of Torah") is a Jewish holiday that celebrates the gift of Torah, and specifically the conclusion of the annual cycle of Torah readings.

Chapter 3

Name

1.

The word "Name" is, as it were, the A of the biblical ABCs, the first and decisive line in the design of the thoughts of God. In the building of scriptural vocabulary, it is the cornerstone, and it possesses a miraculous supporting capacity. It binds even the most disparate parts together and gives these contradictions a gleam of certainty that has no human origin. Whoever learns to fathom this word becomes truly *Bible-believing*.

We might envy bygone times for their "Bible-believing" people, who sat in church and led exemplary lives by word and deed. But it seems that "Bible-believing" has taken on a different meaning in our time, or at least a different color. Sound knowledge now means knowledge of the *grondwoorden*, ground-words, and their import—and not whether or not one knows many texts by heart or how to put them to correct use, enviable as those skills may be. "Bible-believing" in the most important sense suggests someone who has learned the *anti-pagan* and *anti-religious* character of the Bible in its simplest words, which are shared across the most diverse parts of Scripture and illuminate its unity. Whoever understands the *meaning* of "Name," "righteous," "holy," "flesh," "spirit," "world," "age," and learns to spell these words spiritually, this person can read a little independently; they know what they are doing when they read the Bible. To be sure, these words concern only that which is external—external relative to, say, the participation of the soul. But in this booklet, the external takes center stage. Also, as knowledge of this specific object, Scripture, what is external need not be superficial in the least.

2.

These words did not fall from heaven. They are, instead, rooted in a language and a way of life that is originally *pagan*, that is, natural, universally human, generically religious; this goes without saying.

"Pagan" is synonymous with the biblical *goyim* or "peoples." Pagan religion = *Volksreligion* = natural knowledge of God, the religion of the nations, which is to say, the world apart from the "Name" that is the Revelation.

This is why in the Bible not one pivotal word, image, or concept means what it *appears* to mean—what it means in the eyes of pagans, in the eyes of any of us according to our natural thinking and feeling. The prophetic spirit in Israel has bent the words, images, and concepts in order to give witness within the human condition to the wholly Other in its Relation, appointed by God, with humankind.

And the spirit that understands this spirit discovers time and again that the words mean what they naturally mean and also, at the same time, they express something totally different.

If we pay attention to the word

NAME.

3.

The Name *distinguishes* God *from other beings*, gods, and demons. The Bible does not reckon with a general concept of God, only later to add specific names, images, and qualities. The text speaks first and foremost about God as *one* god among other gods. No matter how strange this might sound to us, how primitive it may appear, we cannot pass over this fact, because this primitivity harbors a secret. Old Testament names express something about the essence and destiny of their recipients: Eve, the mother of all the living, Cain, the begotten one, Seth, the stem cutting, Jacob, the heel-catcher, Israel, ruler of God, Moses, drawn out of the water of death. A close relationship exists between changes of name and changes of life and essence: Abram-Abraham (Gen 17:5), Naomi-Mara (Ruth 1:20), Simon-Peter (Mark 3:16), and others. In the same way, an intimate relationship exists between God and the Name (Lev 18:21; Ps 86:11; Exod 15:3; Isa 47:4; 1 Chr 16:10; Ps 105:3). Yes, in the end, the Name is *God's self*, as God reveals that self in a certain, definite relationship to earthly reality. God's Name dwells in the angel (Exod 23:20), dwells in the temple (2 Chr 20:9; 33:4), dwells in the artist (Exod 31:3).

For this reason it is a terrible offense to slander, defame, or abuse that Name (Exod 20:7; Lev 18:21; 19:12; 24:11). Therefore this Name should be known, narrated, feared, loved, confessed, sought, expected, called upon, and sanctified (Deut 28:58; 1 Kgs 8:33; Pss 5:12; 34:4; 52:11; 83:17; 122:4; Isa 26:8; Matt 6:9; John 12:28, etc).

NAME IS REVELATION

The central place of the Name means that revelation is always a *particular* revelation—always has been, is, and will be. God has a name; God is not the nameless one. God is not the All, but is known as a reality that distinguishes itself *in* the world *from* the world. God does not appear to us as the most general, that which can be found everywhere, but rather as the most unique, that which can be sought and found somewhere specific. This does not mean God couldn't *be* the most general and the all-powerful and the omnipresent, but rather that the road to knowledge does not begin with the general. We must follow this road, the road of Revelation, to meet the true and living Godhead.

NAME IS: A GODHEAD WHO HAS BECOME "A" GOD IN ORDER TO BE KNOWN TO HUMANITY

The first commandment is the corollary: You shall have no *other* gods before me. They are there, but they are not *yours*.

3a.

Name denotes in the second place the *addressability* of God, which defines and determines the nature of community. In accordance with Oriental thinking, the name conveys the essence of a thing; the name brings the essence within reach, within the sphere of human influence. One can address the name, invoke it, swear by it, exercise influence with it, acquire power through it. Living religion calls God by name and feels itself called by name.

Thus it is among the pagans, the nations. Thus it is also, formally at any rate, in Israel and the church. But here the Name encloses the absolute power of salvation. Within this covering dwells the everlasting will to save. This Name is named to us, and we name this Name. God has called upon people; now people call upon God. Like a trail of light, now here and now there, the word pierces the speechlessness of the cosmos. It flashes from particular revelation to the particular prayer responding to it.

4.

Whether there is only *one* God is a question of *secondary* importance. But that *this* God is *our* God—herein lies our salvation. It is also the subject of the Bible, which recounts the nature and character and quality of God in God's true and faithful self-revelation to us. *Nowhere* does the Bible speak of God's *essence* in abstracto. Nowhere does it indicate the unity of God in such a way that we may speak of it, except on the basis of the Name. We may learn what unity means here only *by virtue of* the Name. This "detour" is the shortest way toward gaining a sense of who the One and Only and Eternal is. Whoever refuses to take this detour and wishes to proceed directly to the practice of spiritual life will lose their way—in the howling wilderness and the utter emptiness of an isolated, phantasmal understanding. At last, finding themselves in an empty, ghostly world, their will to live will ebb. Israel's contribution to humanity is instead to acknowledge, to confess, and to declare that "this God is our God."

MONOTHEISM IS NOT SPECIAL

because it does not need particular revelation. What is more advanced than monotheism appears in the guise of what is lesser: a god. Next to Baal and others, against Baal but still *next to* Baal, YHWH appears as *a* god who entered into history with divine deliverance and guidance, divine promise and commandment. On this basis, God speaks to the people of God: you shall have *no other gods* before My Countenance. The command does not deny the existence of other gods; it does not contemplate their character, nor measure their power. Whether or not these gods are objective realities or subjective figments of the mind will become clear later on. For now what matters—and what would show the imprint of revelation on our lives—is that these gods, regardless of their power and might, are *not* our gods. Listen to the following sentences:

God has taken his place in the divine council;
    in the midst of the gods he holds judgement (Ps 82:1).

There is none like you among the gods (Ps 86:8).

The Lord is a great King above all gods (Ps 95:3).

Before the gods I sing your praise (Ps 138:1).

The God of gods speaks and summons the earth (Ps 50:1).

Give thanks to the God of gods! (Ps 136:2)

Although the prophets and apostles had long known of the Unity and Singularity of God, the issue received no special emphasis, even including the New Testament. Paul writes thus:

> Even though there may be so-called gods in heaven or on earth—as in fact there are many gods and many lords, yet for *us* there is one God, the Father, from whom are all things and *for whom* we exist, and one Lord, Jesus Christ, through whom are all things and *through whom* we exist (1 Cor 8:5–6).

This is the same *structure* as the Old Testament, which is, to speak, the

METHOD OF THE NAME

namely: first, this God is *our* God—and only then: *this* God is the only, the almighty, the omnipresent, and so on.

4a.

To make this second point perfectly clear: whether only one God is thinkable is a question of secondary importance. But that this God wills to be known in this way, to be called upon and approached like so—*that* is decisive for the whole of human existence. In and with the Name is the vast mystery of prayer at stake. Spinoza was one of the first from Israel to deny God's addressability, and as a consequence, he was excommunicated from the synagogue, which is rightly called the "house of prayer." Spinoza, the great apostate, taught that the person who loves God cannot expect to be loved back by God. "The intellectual love of the mind towards God is the very love with which He loves Himself."[1] Such an idea suspends the Name. It destroys prayer, and it reinstates the muteness of the cosmos—the inhumane, primordial silence before the Name revealed itself.

PRAYER HAS POWER

bestowed by *this* God and authorized by the *Name*. The saying applies to prayer: whoever seeks, finds; whoever asks, "takes"; whoever knocks, to them the door opens (Luke 11:10). All this would not be possible if we had to deal with what is undefined and boundless. Our eyes do not have to wander into vagueness, they need not hover about in space. "Upward I lift mine eyes, from God is all my aid" (Ps 25:7).[2] We look to the form of God's Revelation, upward to the Name. God gives space to our innermost desire, as long as it accords with the "mind of the Spirit" (Rom 8:27).

The Name is revelation, in distinction from that which is "given." At the same time, the Name is meant for use—to name. In just this way, the Name is not empty, and those who call upon the Name do not act in vain.

5.

Take notice of the following words and phrases:

In every place where I cause my name to be remembered (Exod 20:24).

Call on the name of the Lord (for example in Gen 21:33).

O Lord, our Sovereign,
  how majestic is your name in all the earth! (Ps 8:1).

You shall not make wrongful use of the name of the Lord *your* God (Exod 20:7).

The name of the Lord is a strong tower; the righteous run into it and are safe (Prov 18:10).

I have made your name known to those whom you gave me from the world (John 17:6).

On that day the Lord will be one and his name one (Zech 14:9).

There is no other name under heaven given among mortals by which we must be saved (Acts 4:12)

Give me an undivided heart to revere your name (Ps 86:11).

Your name and your renown
  are the soul's desire (Isa 26:8).

Through you alone we acknowledge your name (Isa 26:13, NRSV, adapt.)

6.

It would be too simple and direct for us to make a formal equation of the Name and Revelation. Although this formula is completely true and indispensable for the reading lesson of the biblical ABCs, we still require a more precise and concrete definition. The *context of biblical texts* can indicate for us which specifications are necessary: so, for example, to "speak in the Name" means to speak on the basis of the Revelation. To "pray in the Name" means to plead on the Revelation. "For where two or three are gathered in my Name" (Matt 18:20)—which is to say, in obedience to the Revelation that took place in me, and in expectation of the Revelation that is coming. "In the Name"—this phrase can express multiple relations: grounded in the Revelation, appealing to it, referencing it, expecting it, adhering to it, submitting to it, trusting it through the authority hidden by it, guaranteed by it. The accent of the word itself shifts, since the particular Revelation faces sometimes toward promise and other times toward commandment. It exercises power but is, on the other hand, powerless according to the ways of the world. The Name is at rest; it dwells (Deut 12:11), but it is also coming (Ps 72:19). It is articulate and yet will become even clearer. It happened, happens, and will happen again.

6a.

The exact meaning of the Name changes with context. This is a sign of the humanity and the proximity of the Name. Lest we misuse the Name, however, by flattening it, we must remember at all times that the Name is the Name of *God*: indeed God is the turning of God's own *self* through divine goodness toward the creature. "Spiritual life," "prayer life," and similar expressions carry with them a precarious familiarity. The Name is particular; one should never *get used to this*, that God is different from the gods. Instead, we should rejoice over this particularity with new joy whenever our need propels us toward God. We live by remembrance and by hope; our own religiosity subsists between these two, knowing as we do that our normal respiration cannot survive the high altitudes of this particular knowledge—of this particular God.

7.

Someone is *Bible-believing* when they realize that all the richness and depth of Scripture depends on the holy, most glorious, unsurpassed Name. If we consider the Name to be in the *middle*, only then do we rightly view creation "in the beginning" and salvation "in the last days." We know about both creation and salvation solely through the Name. Once this insight is hammered into a person as a living certainty, once it becomes a strong kernel of knowledge, then we may call them Bible-believing. In our darkest hour when the stars of humanity and culture go out, this certainty will not perish. "For I know that my Redeemer lives" (Job 19:25); "For *I am convinced* that nothing will be able to separate us from the love of God" (Rom 8:38–39). This knowledge and this conviction cannot rest on the general God, the so-called Creator, the self-evident "Providence," but only on the knowledge of the Name of the Lord.

Let us consider some of the consequences of this reasoning:

OUTLOOK

a

We take the structure of Scripture seriously by spelling it out. The revelation to which Scripture gives witness, which it mediates, is distinct from all *paganism*. God is not Nature. God is for *us*, firstly, "smaller"—a quality that we understand makes God greater and more glorious than the ALL. The fact that we know God by and in the Name prevents us from believing in "power in itself," "actuality in itself," "death in itself." All these realities do not "speak" to us, insofar as we learn to believe and trust the holy Teaching about the Name.

b

In just this way is *natural theology* jeopardized. God cannot be equated with Nature, but neither can God be known first and foremost as the Creator of Nature. Belief in the Creator follows from faith in the Name. God's general guidance of the world is known from particular divine acts in history—in holy history. The fixed pattern of Revelation shows itself in this fact: in reading from the particular to the general.

c

This A of the biblical ABCs effectively fences off the danger that theology would merge into *philosophy*, preaching into argumentation, faith into worldview, the command of God into human morality, promise into ideal. Even if we are tempted to transgress, and even if it is perhaps somewhat unavoidable to think and speak in a philosophical or moralistic way, the Name always calls us to remember anew the order that governs the world of the particular revelation.

d

The meaning of speaking *anthropomorphically* becomes clearer now. Anthropomorphic speech about God should not be excused away as a product of our limited, human mind, and so on. It should rather be justified by appeal to the Name: the form that God takes in Self-Revelation. On the basis of the Name we know that the human form that God has chosen, sanctified, and blessed comes far nearer to the reality of God than the forms of nature, or images modeled on impersonal entities like the Absolute, the Infinite, the eternal Power, the eternal Silence, the Vastness, or the Abyss. God, *this* God, has human features, and therein we encounter the divinity of this God, the divinity of the Name.

Humanity remains the sign and seal of the true Divinity of the Lord. Know that the *Lord* is the Godhead (Ps 100:3).

The world, indeed the earth itself suggests to us the concepts of "infinity" and "eternity." From there our chaotic (and, secretly, already melancholic) longings arise, the wanderlust and urge toward death and unrest, which artists overcome in order to arrive at form and shape. Form and shape are confinements. If the *Name* of God is anthropomorphic and not formed from nature, it means that we can be healed of our undetermined longings and borderless urges; as humans, then, we can turn back to the message of the One who has taken on human form.

NOTES

1. Baruch Spinoza, *Ethics*, trans. W.H. White, rev. A.H. Stirling, Wordsworth Classics of World Literature (Ware: Wordsworth, 2001), 80.

2. Miskotte here quotes from the Dutch rhymed Psalter of 1773; our English version is therefore correspondingly excerpted from Isaac Watts's hymn, "God Our Preserver."

Chapter 4

The Names of God

1.

The names of God are distinguished from the Name. We need to get used to this distinction in order to read Scripture properly. Scripture contains a multiplicity of names, and at times the boundary between a permanent name and a passing form of address cannot be drawn with certainty. If reading is indeed bending under the Teaching, this also means that we learn to join ourselves under the *one* Name, which is Revelation itself. The Name is the total expression of God's being, while the various names of God summarize particular aspects, tendencies, and meanings of the *one* Name: the Mighty One, God Most High, the Lord of Hosts, the Holy One of Israel, the Deliverer, the Savior, the Creator, and all the other names that could be mentioned here. These form a procession and an escort around the actual revelation.

2.

The Name is rooted in one name of God. This name is a mysterious sign, continually providing food for thought. It is the name YHWH, Yahweh, Jehovah, best rendered as "I will be with you as I will be with you" (Exod 3:14). This means that (a) God has revealed the divine self in this way and (b) God reveals that humans (Moses, Israel, the church) are called and elected to name this name. Paganism projects divine names out of their experience of life in the world: Zeus or Odin, the All, Life, Fate. But humans cannot *seize* the knowledge of God; it must be given to them. Such knowledge is given through encounter: through relationship, or "covenant." This name of God is the anti-pagan monument par excellence; it is the cornerstone upon which all philosophical endeavor stumbles. The other names of God come more or less spontaneously to our lips, but the covenant name of YHWH is put by YHWH on our lips. "This is my name for ever, and this my title for all generations" (Exod 3:15b). All the names and virtues of God are anchored in this mystery; that the entirety of God's saving deeds are grounded in God's holy decision to be known by this name into the future and unto the end of the age.

3.

The name has taken shape in one human life: a total human life has become, without remainder, revelation. Jesus Christ is the Name through which we know all that we were given to know. Through him we may look backward and forward to recognize the whole of God's work in the world *as salvation.*

The essence of salvation is this: that God is a "human" God, in contrast with the gods of the pagans and the godhead of ancient and modern naturalism. God has become human. All of God's revelation is aligned toward humankind, so that we might have access to God. The human form of revelation enables all of us, from every tongue and tribe and people and nation, to approach this "human" God with boldness and unshakeable trust: a God who is so much "smaller" than the All. Such a God seems to be "just a human," but precisely in that form God unmasks the gods of the All as inhuman, grotesque demons.

"The eternal Good is your brother!" Luther sang.[1]

3a.

In this way, the name

JESUS CHRIST

is the *fulfillment, confirmation, and perpetuation* of the *one* name of God, YHWH.

This means

a that Christianity can never be a new religion;
b that the New Covenant is the fulfillment of the Old, but that the New Testament as *writing* is a commentary on the Old Testament;
c that "I will be with you, as I will be with you" indicates the sovereign power of the Name, but also and by the same token, faithfulness itself: "See, I am with you always, to the end of the age" (Matt 28:20).

The biblical ABCs—which is to say, the simplest configuration of words, their fundamental order—specify this equation: Name = Revelation; name = YHWH, name = Jesus Christ. Even the most perceptive dogmatic treatise, exercising all powers of distinction, could never totally succeed in probing this relationship, and yet it lies open to every person who reads the Bible as Teaching: as holy Instruction to accompany us through life.

4.

From this epicenter we may read and listen to the other names of God that Scripture uses.

The whole of salvation history belongs to the *Name*, that is, to the revelation. The word and the event, the promise and the commandment, the works and the wonders: the *unity* of all these is summarized in the Name YHWH, and this Name is "fulfilled" in the name Jesus Christ. And "there is *no other name* under heaven given among mortals by which we must be saved" (Acts 4:12). This name is hence identical with the Name of which it was said, "this is my name for ever, and this my title for all generations" (Exod 3:15b).

Therefore the root and essence of the Name lies in the form of the *one* and in the content of the other. Taken together they constitute the widest and most world-comprehending, the most nations-ruling and future-opening reality:

The Revelation!

The other names of God surround, accompany, and illuminate this essence, but fragmentarily. As such, each fragment can only be understood by starting with *the* Name and moving outwards from that epicenter.

5.

Elohim = "God" appears so commonly in the Bible as a word for God that it almost nowhere gives the impression of being a proper name; it functions instead like a common noun. We are thus naturally inclined to consider YHWH as a more or less acceptable epithet for this aforementioned, generic designation, "God." But the word Elohim—literally meaning gods, divinity, pleroma, godhead, and usually paired with a singular verb (as, for example, in Gen 1:1: "in the beginning gods created")—might seduce us in just this fashion. But no! Our learning of the biblical ABCs has put us on the alert. We know that *Elohim, too, should be heard as a proper name*, and indeed in connection with and in light of the *one*, comprehensive Name that has been given to us. This God YHWH, *this one* is Elohim! The Name has a fullness of life, thought, and power, whose limit is beyond our sight. When we wish to express *this* dimension of the Name, we call God *Elohim*, the Godhead. We do not proceed like this: first entertaining a general, self-evident idea about divinity and then supplementing, expanding, or explaining it through the particular Name of God. On the contrary, we move from the singular, specific God toward a confession of Godhead. "Know that the Lord is Godhead" (Ps 100:3).

6.

El Shaddai is usually translated "God Almighty," but it actually means "God of the mountain," which is to say: God of the world, of the future: God who reigns over the future by a divine miracle. It will not do to equate this name with the name *Creator*, and nor even to place it in relationship to *Creator* without qualification. *El Shaddai* does not betoken some general power, but a particular power: namely, the Power that brought about Isaac's miraculous birth from the shriveled loins of Abraham and the barren womb of Sarah—and through them, the entire chosen people.

The people so blessed called God El Shaddai. But when seen within the whole of Scripture and taken within the language of the Bible, El Shaddai becomes an *aspect*, a luminous *aspect*, of the Name that is Revelation itself.

YHWH, the nameless Name, the revealed and hidden Name, comprehends this aspect, too: *the exercise of power against death*. This God negates the fatality of nature and suspends the consequences that accrue to our human lives: "the God who gives life to the dead and calls into existence the things that do not exist" (Rom 4:17). If we wish to emphasize this facet of the *one* Name, we call God El Shaddai. El Shaddai appears as a negative expression, as of unchecked power, only in the disputes of the despairing Job; the same book features the holy Name YHWH twice only, in the prologue and epilogue. This suggests that there is no salvation or meaning in the divine power unless it is the divine power of *this* one, whose name means, "I will be with you." To consider that this One holds all power, including the power over everything that happens to us, even "omnipotence"—to consider that even death is no limit to this God—such considerations lead to thanksgiving, just like the patriarchs rendered to God.

7.

The Lord of Hosts—in a surprising way, this name at once means "Lord of angels," "Lord of stars," and "Lord of Israel's military forces." It, too, should be included as a part of the biblical ABCs. With this name the *one* Name is explained as the God of *history*, who takes no rest before the final victory is fought. God is more the god of history than the god of nature. Nature is the ground, the basis, the structure; but history is the location, the human drama, in which God performs divine acts. And *God is not alone in this*, but is surrounded and reinforced by hosts—by legions of seraphs and cherubs, archangels, thrones, powers, messengers, with whom God shares divine power to bless and to guide, so that they might serve God's purpose. The Lord of Hosts "surrounds himself" with the power of judges, the heroes (Judg 6:34). God deputizes the rulers of the world (Cyrus of Persia is called God's *messiah* or "anointed one," destined for a particular service within world history, Isa 45:1).

> Who is the King of glory?
>   The Lord, strong and mighty . . .
> The Lord of Hosts,
>   he is the King of glory (Ps 24:8a, 10b).

> See what desolations he has brought on the earth.
> He makes wars cease to the end of the earth;
>   he breaks the bow, and shatters the spear;
>   he burns the shields with fire . . .
> The Lord of Hosts is with us (Ps 46:8b–9, 11a).

Here, too, it remains of utmost importance for correct reading that we remember and apply our knowledge of the *grondstructuur*, the ground structure. The Warrior, the Commander, the Sovereign of history—who is this One? Can we find out by scrutinizing history for what happened and what is happening, which things failed and which things succeeded, which feats endured and which perished quickly? No. We do not call the "Lord of history" YHWH or other titles, but rather, the other way around: we name YHWH and no other, a particular God with particular virtues and definite intentions, and to this one we also add, among other titles, the Lord of History: *YHWH Sebaoth*, the Lord of Hosts.

8.

The Father—this is what God is called in the Old Testament (e.g., in Ps 103:12; Isa 63:16; 64:8). God is the Father especially of the king, the Messiah, and of those with messianic features, which they carried as forerunners and signs, whether personally or as a function of their office (Ps 2:7, 12).

And finally, *Father* is the name that describes the most intimate confession of the Name in the Christian congregation. There among the congregation is the Spirit, through whom we call out: *Abba! Father!* (Rom 8:15). There, too, is the Our Father prayed. And still this name is not more or higher or wider than the Name itself, the Revelation, "the only name under heaven given among mortals by which we must be saved" (Acts 4:12). We would therefore fracture the integrity of Scripture if we even for one moment succumb to our inclination to play the old game: to proceed from what is known, from what is known to *us*, and to say: the Father! well, that is of course the Creator or the real Godhead, and "we are all children of one Father."[2] God is called *Father* primarily in view of God's eternal relationship to the *Son*, Jesus Christ. Jesus first appeared, and only then did we hear about the Father as *his Father* (and through him, *our* Father). Reversing the biblical *order* and defying the ABCs is perhaps in no place more fatal to the security, joy, and resilience of our lives. To speak with the greatest clarity: Father is more truly an *epithet* of the Name than the reverse, according to which the Name and its root, YHWH, would be an epithet or clarifying addendum to the name Father which we already know. The *Lord* is *also* called Father, in the same way that God may be called the Mighty One, the Lord of Hosts, the Godhead, just is this *Same One* is called, addressed, and confessed as *Son* and *Spirit*—but this is too broad a territory to cross at this time. Who is the one who is called "Father"? That is the

ONE AND ONLY,

whom we know through the particular revelation. *Father* expresses that what radiates toward us in Jesus Christ is not just a historical phenomenon or some contingent event; not an incomprehensible high point of religion or human achievement; nor yet an ecstatic creation of humans, genies, angels or archangels. On the contrary, it expresses that the One who is with us and for us in Jesus Christ also lives in the heavens: in the depths of divine constancy and faithfulness. Against the appearance of chance and relativity, against the violence of demonic reality, against the tribulation of our oppressed spirit and agonized mind, we now confess the Name. We confess *Jesus* in that we call upon and testify to

ABBA, FATHER.

We do not first confess the Father and then supplement it by confessing the Son. Quite the opposite: Father! becomes a proper name, a name to invoke and "cry out" (Rom 8:15) by virtue of the name Jesus and on the basis of the Revelation that occurred in him. In this same way do we understand the other, more incidental names, though we do not discuss them here: Adonai, the Lord; the Holy One of Israel, and so on, as well as *compound names*: the Lord God, the Lord of Lords (i.e., the Lord, whom we call YHWH), some of which continue into the New Testament (Luke 1:16; Acts 7:37; 1 Pet 3:15; Rev 1:8; 22:5).

We understand further how the *Pantocrator*, "the All-powerful" functions in apposition to the holy Name (Rev 4:8; 11:17; 15:3; 16:7; 21:22). We even find confirmation in the world of the *goyim*, the nations or *pagans*, in the realm that we call world history and politics: nothing is too wonderful for the Lord (Jer 32:17).

Everything has its ordained time, and everything in the biblical ABCs has its ordained place; if we find it there in God's timing, it appears to be a treasure, a jewel of wisdom, a pledge of love.

NOTES

1. Miskotte probably refers to Luther's hymn, "Gelobet seist du, Jesu Christ" (English: "All Praise, Lord Jesus Christ, to Thee"). The second stanza reads: "Th' eternal Father's only Son Now is in the manger found / And so in our poor flesh and blood, Is now arrayed th' eternal Good."

2. Miskotte quotes from a well-known Dutch hymn written by Catharina van Rennes (1858–1940).

Chapter 5

The Order of God's Virtues

1.

We read the Bible in order to understand the Teaching, and we desire to understand the Teaching in order to know the Name.

Before proceeding, and especially here just before the content grows more difficult, it would be helpful to remind ourselves that reading needs to change into *hearing*, and hearing into the obedience of faith. Therefore: a short excursus about reading as such.

Reading remains a hazardous endeavor; it shares the danger that accompanies every solitary activity. While reading, we quickly find ourselves *in a closed world*: a world of pictures that quite pleases us. But this world of pictures is very much *our* world. And the power of the word is also unique among art forms: it impresses reality vividly upon us, and it can be sung, and painted, and it also, furthermore, participates in the Logos: in reason or understanding. What Victor Hugo described by hyperbole is not, after all, an accident of cultural history: *ceci tuera cela*—"this here [the book] will kill that [the cathedral]."[1] The book is the essence of the age: the thought of the times, distilled down and available to the solitary person. The word *book* has therefore acquired a normative character. But not everything that appears outwardly as a book is a *book* in this sense.

Books exist that *are less than a book, as, for example, a grammar. Then there are books that are books*, as, for example, Goethe's *Wilhelm Meister*. And there are books that are more than books, as, for example, a tragedy like Hamlet, which needs to be acted on stage. A book is a world subsisting in itself. Its form and content are one, such that its parts balance each other, and, like stones in an arch, they do not require outside support. *The Bible is not this kind of book*. It doesn't exist to be read in solitude, but rather to be read aloud. Throughout the times of the Old and New Testaments and during all of European church history—up until the era of the printing press—Scripture functioned in a world of illiteracy. Scripture is meant to be read, yes: to be read *aloud*. Scripture is meant for humans, yes: yet not for the solitary human, but for the community: the congregation, the gathering in the synagogue, in the church, on the mission field. Scripture announces that it must be *heard* spiritually, in that it does not reveal its essence as a book. Instead, it is *more* than a book, and as a result, it must be heard, literally speaking, as a *chant*. The Hebrew cantor and the Roman priest and the Saxon farmer and the Polish Hasid modulate, rhythmicize, scan: they perform the text as a song, as liturgical saying, as prayer, as divine pronouncement, as proclamation for this day and hour.

What does all of this have to say to us, and what is the connection with the biblical ABCs? It means this: that even as we need an ABC presentation of the basic elements of biblical language, we should still bear in mind that these elements are not closed forms. They act as *instruments* of the Truth, which takes them up and uses them so fiercely that they bend and nearly burst open under this abnormal pressure. The Bible is, in the final analysis, about the content or *Sache* and not about the words. The Spirit that places the words does not place them as words of a book but as words of life.

Nevertheless, only the *oer-woorden* or primary words make the words of life into the words for our life.

We must also learn—so wondrous is this book—that a particular *order* governs it; the Bible is marked out by a definite language. On the other hand, we must reckon with the independence and sovereignty of its essential subject matter or *Sache*, who is a *Person*: an Actor, an Author, a Speaker, a Leader, who takes up and sanctifies our images for a specific service. This One is also able to replace or supplement them, or even to drop them entirely, if we become engrossed in the book instead of opening ourselves under the Word.

2.

The biblical ABCs slow down and moderate our inclination to become absorbed, for instance, in the Name, because they draw attention to the *adjectives* associated with it. For alongside the Name as a noun stand the properties or virtues of God, expressed as adjectival descriptors. This holds true not only in a literal but also in a spiritual sense. Great and dreadful, righteous and gracious, merciful and holy, jealous (Exod 20:5) and faithful, longsuffering and truthful, enraged and wise—we are not permitted to understand them as "anthropomorphic" images of something that is in itself completely different. Even though it *is* something completely different—as, for example, God's righteousness and our righteousness—it is not so different that these adjectives cannot indicate it.

To hear the Name correctly, we need to know that it already contains all the *virtues* of God—the divine perfections of the Eternal One. But this holds true the other way around as well: to know that the Name contains all God's virtues, we need to understand the adjectives correctly, since they refer to these virtues.

3.

So we want to read the Bible. We want to learn from the Torah. We want to try reading in a way that turns around into hearing—and then we encounter, for example, a *narrative* like the conquest of Canaan. To begin with, this is clearly not a teaching about some generic God, but the story of a very specific God: it is a teaching about the Name. And yet the aspect of the Name that these texts reveal is . . . *horrifying*. Are we speaking correctly, then, if we say: therefore the Lord is a horrifying God, as if this is a stable connection, a permanent title, or a fixed epithet? No! Every quality, every "virtue" of the Name is the Name itself, not only in a particular way of being (e.g., as in the Lord of Hosts), but also in its concrete application. The Name is so rich that the adjective "horrifying" needs to be juxtaposed to it. The point is not to evoke one or another horror, like that of a volcano eruption, or that of a tyrant, or of a witch—no, the meaning of the descriptor cannot be considered on its own as if were a noun. The content of the adjective cannot be allowed to overgrow the noun in our understanding. Rather, this adjective communicates the horrifying aspect of *this* God, whose Name we know, and to whose Name other adjectives equally belong: adjectives like holy, righteous, wise, and merciful. This same relation pertains to other biblical texts, too: in a *narrative* of deliverance and liberation, or in the case of a psalm, a proverb, or a parable. In all these instances, any given adjective speaks truthfully with regard to God—but at the same time, its truthfulness is only relative. It is truthful insofar as it unfolds the Name, but it is relative because it addresses no more than one concrete manifestation of the Name. We must think in this way about all the *oerwoorden* or primary words that articulate the virtues of God, and negotiate them accordingly. They clarify each other; they illuminate and support, delimit and define each other. And yet they do not do so *arbitrarily*, as if they were completely interchangeable with one another. There is an

ORDER OF VIRTUES

which we must not deny, because understanding it belongs to the biblical ABCs.

3a.

Before we clarify this point, another aspect of these adjectives deserves attention: namely, their *illuminating* and *revealing* function. This role is necessary for us humans, since we are, by nature, pagan. Some though not all of the adjectives mentioned above are *pleonasms*. They are, in some sense, redundant. So, for example, we already speak about a punctilious civil servant, or a sharp thinker, or a faithful spouse, without recognizing that by adding each of these adjectives, we devalue and discredit the corresponding noun. Our use of the phrase "righteous God" is a poignant proof of our constant need—as pagans—for such an adjective and reminder. In and of itself, the expression "righteous YHWH" is nonsensical and redundant, because the Name already fully encloses righteousness. And yet in view of our penchant for understanding the Name in an abstract sense as "Godhead in general," the circumlocution of divine attributes is

NOT SUPERFLUOUS.

Specifying the divine virtues is, for us, a precaution: a preventative measure intended to preempt our disposition toward religion and to intercept our pagan thinking. To pronounce the very high and spiritual idea that the world is "an essential component in the life of God"[2] is just as pagan as primitive animism. It nullifies the Name and upends the order of virtues.

4.

By referring to the *order* of attributes or virtues, we mean an *order-for-us*: a sequence in our cognizance and experience, and therefore a sequence for our confession and praise and vitality. If we haphazardly order the concepts of omnipotence, grace, omniscience, righteousness, and wisdom, because we feel no particular order or sense of priority—all the while believing that we are rightly speaking and praying and loving—accidents are bound to happen. Knowing the *way* that we humans come to the saving knowledge of God—which is to say, *the Name* of God—belongs to the biblical ABCs. Such knowing is not a one-time event but a continuous renewal, through which our joy may remain.

5.

Everything therefore hinges on the question of whether we are *leaving our paganism*.

Many gods are well-known: namely, as rulers and benefactors over certain areas or territories. But in the pagan understanding, "God" means an X: a blank. The sum total of all the known gods turns out to be, oddly enough . . . the Unknown. For Israel and for the church, God is not an X, but the Name, the named Lord. And that Name is rich, an overflowing world in which to live. The holy Teaching leads us into the Name. The Name encompasses God's Virtues and God's Acts; everything that the Bible contains spells out for us this Name together with its virtues and acts. The story of the Exodus and the story of the Exile and the story of Jesus's earthly life, the commandments, the sacrificial regulations, the lamentations—together, they all recount the Name, because together, they are *teaching*. This instruction is good and beautiful and in a whole life long, we will not exhaust it.

And *yet*, the beauty of this teaching falls into *disarray*, and its goodness becomes *harmful*, if we do not hold fast to the Name by observing the order of the virtues.

If we adhere to this order, we will stay close to the particularity of the Name. We will not then want for light or consolation or anticipation of the eternal future. But if we fail to hold onto this order, God, the Lord, becomes once more an X. We won't then know if we can count on such a Name; all divine virtues come unmoored, all divine acts appear as incursions of an unknown energy, and the Lord reduces to a projection of our human—which is to say, pagan—experience of life.

6.

Please bear this in mind and learn it by heart!
These *three*

REVERSALS OF THE ORDER:

a When we proceed from *infinitude*, we distort the knowledge of God's name, because we cancel out a priori the veracity of divine *encounters*.
b When we proceed from *omnipotence*, we distort the knowledge of God's name, because we make no space for divine *acts* of mercy and righteousness.
c When we proceed from the equivalency of the so-called communicable attributes of God, for example, righteousness and mercy, we vacate the appearance of *Jesus Christ*.

6a.

Just as the Name signifies a particular revelation, God's eternity means the particular eternity of *this* God, and omnipotence indicates the omnipotence of *this God*. As such, omnipotence entails a particular kind of power over all, which we have come to know, not by inference from the ALL, but through *this* One: through the appearance of Jesus Christ. In the being and counsel of *this* God, no equivalency is possible between righteousness and mercy. "Grace abounded all the more" (Rom 5:20).

The infinitude of which the holy Teaching speaks does not drive our thoughts toward an X: a blank.

The omnipotence of which the holy Teaching speaks does not bend us down beneath an X-fate.

The grace of which the holy Teaching speaks does not entice us into some game of chance in which we might find that judgment rather than grace is the meaning of our life.

As if the Name were not trustworthy!

6b.

Like the Name itself, the attributes—the virtues—are proclaimed by the Lord for all time in the moment of divine revelation (Exod 34:6–7).

> The Lord passed before him, and proclaimed, "Lord, Lord, a God merciful and gracious, slow to anger and abounding in steadfast love and faithfulness, keeping steadfast love for the thousandth generation, forgiving iniquity and transgression and sin, yet by no means clearing the guilty, but visiting the iniquity of the parents upon the children."

It would hardly have been the same if the following had been written instead: "Lord, Lord, omnipotent, omniscient, omnipresent . . ."

And neither could the order have been reversed by speaking first about God's righteousness, and only secondly of God's mercy, grace, and faithfulness. Then the virtues would have fallen to pieces. The miracle of the holy Teaching is that it is, in fact, *the other way around*: the omnipotence of the Lord is the power of mercy and grace, the power of patience and faithfulness, the power of retribution and forgiveness. Divine "infinitude" is the *qualitative superabundance* of *this* God's mercy, *this* God's grace; *this* One's faithfulness, retribution, and forgiveness.

7.

Omnipotence as an abstraction does *not*, then, precede; it is *not* necessary, and, finally, it is *not* rational. Therefore,

WE PRAISE THE NAME.

Don't the psalms now come to life for us? With all their urgency to sanctify, to praise, to worship, to lift up, and to magnify the Name?

There, in *song*, the Name appears as wholly particular! Indeed, the Name features as that special mystery from out of which we live, and the seal proving that *this* God is different and entirely other than all gods and everything that is called god.

Such praise is the joy of a soul drenched in wonder that we do not *have to be* pagans any more, that we are

BROUGHT OUT OF THE HOUSE OF BONDAGE, bondage to demons,

and that the holy Teaching prevents us from returning to it. It intercepts that slander and devilish trick, of reducing the Lord to an X: of making God into an Emptiness; a Night; a kind of Demon.

8.

In this time of the disenchantment of the earth and the revelation of the abyss above us and below us, and devoid of light—we are beginning to perceive so-called theological *enlargements* afresh. These enlargements were undertaken because the Name was considered too "narrow-minded." But such enhancements—concepts like infinitude and omniscience and law—disjoin and discourage our soul. They expel us and condemn us, unless we accept the particular virtues of *this* particularly revealed God. In that event, infinitude is shown to be demonic in the same way as the most dreadful African mask.[3] Omnipotence appears to us like the head of a Gorgon, and Law in the abstract, like the indiscriminate firing of a machine gun.

> O God, the insolent rise up against me;
> a band of ruffians seeks my life . . .
> *But you*, O Lord, are a God merciful and gracious,
> slow to anger and abounding in steadfast love and truth (Ps 86:14–15, NRSV adapt.; cf. Ps 103:7ff; Ps 145:8ff).

> Why do you boast, O mighty one,
>   of mischief done . . . all day long!
> but I will thank you forever,
>   because of what you have done (namely, to uproot and snatch him); I will wait on Your Name; for it is good before your saints (Ps 52, various verses, NRSV adapt).

9.

This order lies before us as the *grondpatroon* or ground-pattern of all Scripture. If we don't discern it, that is because we take supposedly self-evident, general categories with us when we approach Scripture. We already know too much; we bring a repertoire of fixed, natural words: for example, "God," "the Godhead," "the All," "the Supreme Being," "the Infinite." We must leave these at home. We can't use them, or at least we can't make a *beginning* with them. So much weight is placed on the Name, and so much weight is placed on the order of the divine attributes. True infinitude is the infinite holiness and grace of *this* God, whose name is YHWH. True omnipotence follows from the end of the holy Teaching: *this* God's power, in particular God's power to bring forth the messianic reign in spite of this world's endless resistance. True justice appears at the end of the holy Teaching: *this* God's jurisdiction, in particular God's right to *acquit* those who are in Christ Jesus.

The same is the case with the *omniscience* and *omnipresence*. First we must know and acknowledge that God knows *something*, in order to know that God knows everything. First we must know and acknowledge that God is *somewhere*, to know that God is everywhere. It is not "naive" thinking that comes to us in Scripture, when it says that God knows this or that human, or that God knows the righteous (Ps 1:6); that God "tests the hearts and kidneys" (Ps 7:9; Jer 17:10; 1 Kgs 8:39); that God knows what is conditional *as* conditional and the contingent *as* contingent (1 Sam 23:10ff; 2 Kgs 13:19; Ps 81:14, Matt 11:21). It is not naive when the Bible says that God goes, comes, walks, descends, and so on, because *this One* is omniscient. This One rules the places of the world by a divine act—with a sequence of divine acts for the sake of the earth.

When we come to understand these things, becoming as naive as the Bible, we perceive that God dwells in the Temple and in Christ; in the church and in the sacrament. Such knowledge does not exclude the general, but rather the other way around. If we proceed from the general, we empty all the names, virtues, and acts of God, and we reduce them to symbols: pale emblems that we could eventually do without and give up. Yes, in the end, in this way, the whole appearance of Christ becomes an illustration of a truth that we already knew by another way.

It is crucial that the "communicable" attributes precede, and the "incommunicable" attributes follow, for the gravity and fervor of our life. This "order of virtues" carries with it the weight of the "sensual" image. Scripture contains imagery and figurative language, and yet these images—though remaining images—are not *merely* images, thanks to the truthfulness of the Name and the order of divine attributes.

God is compared, for example, with an eagle (Deut 32:11), but that means, the way an eagle *acts*; likewise, with a lion (Isa 31:4); with the sun (Ps 84:12); with a candle (Rev 21:23); with a fountain (Ps 36:10); a well or wellspring (Jer 2:13); a mountain range (Deut 32:4); a shield, a shadow, a road, a house.

When we come to imagery drawn from higher beings like humans, it doesn't necessarily entail that its meaning is loftier. It means only that the divine action that such imagery evokes has a deeper impact and yields more clarity: God is a man (Isa 54:5), a groom (Isa 61:10), a warrior (Exod 15:3), a hero (Ps 78:65; Zeph 3:17), an artist and an architect (Heb 11:10), a vine-grower (John 15:1), a shepherd (Ps 23:1), a lawgiver (Isa 33:22).

Conversely, one should not value elements in the holy Teaching less when they feature *lower* images, speaking of God's throne and seat, scepter and rod, God's weapons like bow and arrows, chariot and banners, God's book, God's treasure and God's own inheritance. These images are part of the holy Teaching, and they serve its purpose, namely, to instruct us regarding the Name, which is Revelation. This Name unfolds in the divine attributes, virtues, and perfections.

This is the way the *in*finity, the *omni*potence, and so on of the Lord is proclaimed; these attributes can *for this reason* also be contemplated and praised, not in disruption of the Name, but to confirm the knowledge and glorification of the

LIVING GOD.

A so-called systematic approach, that is, an approach proceeding from a general idea, rooted in natural thinking, would bring the revelation of God into a closed system,

> *destroying* the order
> *darkening* our soul,
> *perplexing* our conscience
> *robbing* us of the joy of salvation,
> *extinguishing* the praise and worship
> of the congregation and the silent
> ecstasy of the individual.

Throughout Scripture as holy instruction, the road of our knowledge runs from the particular to the general, from quality to quantity, from the moment to the outlook of ages, from the particular Name to the Godhead of God, from the particular power, revealed in cross and resurrection, to omnipotence over the world with an eye toward the future, from the particular forms of presence as the following: the Temple, the Word, the Sacrament, to omnipresence; from the particular foreknowledge of election to omniscience. Therefore we are exhorted by the order of the holy Teaching to worship in the song of praise (This alone generates right *praxis*!):

I will extol you, my God and King,
    and bless your name forever and ever.
Every day I will bless you,
    and praise your name forever and ever.
My mouth will speak the praise of the Lord,
    and all flesh will bless his holy name forever and ever (Ps 145:1, 2, 21).

NOTES

1. Victor Hugo (1802–1885), *The Hunchback of Notre Dame*, Book V, chapter 2; in the Wordsworth Classics edition, ed. Keith Wren (Hertfordshire: Wordsworth, 2004), 146.

2. Miskotte quotes from Herman Bavinck's *Reformed Dogmatics, Vol 2: God and Creation*, trans. John Vriend (Grand Rapids: Baker Academic, 2004), 115: "'Without the world God is not God,' the world, therefore, is an essential component in the life of God." Bavinck, whose volume was in Miskotte's library, is quoting Arthur Drews, *Die deutsche Spekulation seit Kant*, 2 vols. (Berlin: P. Maeter, 1893), 1:229, whose book Miskotte did not have.

3. Miskotte uses here a Dutch word that has moved semantically from a more neutral reference to African-descended people (counterpart to English "Negro") to a slur (more like the English N-word): *het schrikkelijkst negermasker*. Regardless the word itself, Miskotte's comparison is an example of the casual racism that he shared with his contemporaries. Our translation avoids the term itself without thereby eliminating the cultural chauvinism of Miskotte's comparison.

Chapter 6

The Unity of God's Virtues

1.

It will be beneficial to briefly introduce this topic as well, though not everyone will grasp its helpfulness at this juncture. We have understood from the preceding chapters that the holy Teaching distinguishes itself spiritually from the speech of other powers by virtue of its untranslatable *grondtaal* or ground-language; perhaps we have also discovered to our surprise the extent to which Scripture is, formally speaking, fit for reading aloud and listening to. Scripture is a "book that is *more* than a book." It is self-contained—and yet it does not *wish* to contain itself. It is, like other books, a world in and unto itself—but not a closed world; rather Scripture reveals *the* world. It is a sign and index of the Name, the Act, the Revelation of God on earth. All *gnosis*, including theology grounded in reason and self-sufficient science, inevitably violates the Name of God, because the Name can never be systematized, even though the Name demonstrates a coherent order of virtues. Not only scholars but many simple folks, too, come under the spell of this gnosis, in spite of the warning and precaution that the preceding chapter presents.

It is therefore necessary to add this topic to these precautions and warning signals.

Teaching is meant for proclamation.

This means that we should keep in mind not only that Scripture is not a work of fiction. It is also a liturgical and cultic writing, to be read aloud at a hundred different occasions and consequently with a *thousand emphases*. As such, Scripture transcends the plane of human intellection, which organizes and labels and parcels according to the measure of common-sense reason;

or of the people; or the nation. It is at least as important to imagine and understand that Scripture is meant for proclamation—and not to proclaim a thousand different things, but rather, *one truth*; or better, *one event*; or better yet, one event with a particular purpose, namely, to announce salvation, to galvanize mission, to make disciples. In short,

TO ESTABLISH COMMUNITIES,

where praise rises up, in song and in deed, in the unity of the Spirit. *This* unity is the reflex and answer to the divine Unity, which sums up the divine perfections and presents them rightly to us as perfections; as virtues.

To our eyes, *multiplicity* precedes *Unity*.

Such unity is a reality in God, but not in our understanding or experience. Through proclamation, however, God's unity becomes a kind of objective power; through confession in word and deed, God's unity is honored as simple and harmonious. This *unity* cannot be seen. It cannot be pieced together from various emphases and facets. Rather, this unity must be *heard*, and not just in the way that one listens to someone reading aloud—but as one hears a declaration of love, or a sentence of death, or an acquittal.

2.

It is perfectly true that the pages of Scripture are not directly proclamation. Already we have heard this truth: proclamation *arises out of* Scripture, while Scripture, as it presents itself to us, should be considered as holy teaching. All the same, we cannot omit the present theme, because the unity of divine virtues is in and of itself no virtue, except that it is the foundation of everything, and nothing else if not the mystery of

DIVINE LOVE.

This Love cannot be described in any teaching, and it cannot be conveyed in narrative form, however sacred it may be; nor can it be expressed by liturgical reading, however variegated it may be. This Love is preached: it can *only* be preached, proclaimed, and exclaimed. And on the human side: accepted, believed, embraced, and experienced. This Love, we are accustomed to saying, is a mystery. Yet that word is insufficient; it is too static and subdued, too substantive, when Love is *event*! It is an event that surpasses all substances and intersects all other events.

This book, however, does not address the content of this Love. One could even say that its whole method is to circumvent the issue, because we do not attend to the content of the teaching, but only to its language and form of teaching (about which a great deal has already been said). If teaching receives so little attention, the present chapter engages the matter of proclamation even less. The chapter does not itself preach, it does not witness, it does not even catechize (that would concern the *contents* of the teaching). Instead it treats the alphabet, which is a formal consideration—through which the Bible is spiritually (!) distinguished. This elementary grammar is at most an imprint of the uniqueness of the Name. We do not sit in church, or in a school apart from the church, but rather in the *beit midrash*, the house of learning next to the church, and we have the lectionary before us, with its signposts: teaching, name, virtue, and others.

3.

We emphasize this point because the *unity of the divine virtues* does not, according to the teaching of Scripture, belong to the divine Being as such, but rather to the one Act, which is to say: to the event of God's Love.

We hesitate even to give the impression that we are interpreting divine unity in terms of our ABCs—when that unity is the *presupposition* of all revelation and reconciliation, all names and virtues, all promises and commands; of the divine advent and second coming, of consolation in living and strength in dying, and the *unio mystica*, the mystical union. Only in proclamation and by God's will does the unity of divine virtues—which is Love—make itself known to our heart and to our hidden self. We may *never* assume that the *unity* of God, the *unity* of divine virtues, is described or conveyed anywhere in full. Just like a declaration of love cannot be exhaustively fathomed with words, even less is it possible for us to put into words what *happens* (because it is an event that happens *in* God and *out of* God and *to* God) when Love pours out with generative power, creative light, heavenly spaces, matchless bliss—with absolute authority and consuming force—into human hearts and lives.

4.

What we *can* do, and what exists within the parameters of the biblical ABCs, is to describe the conceptual insights that follow from this presupposition of Love. This can and must happen in the *house of learning*. We will certainly have overcome the childhood challenge of teething that consists in thinking that spelling the ABCs is irreverent—when we move on to adolescent hubris, the gnosis of a closed system. It is after all so simple, this necessity of understanding the Teaching; it is our companion in life. We recognize that such understanding is not the same as receiving the event of Love itself; nevertheless, our true emancipation requires us to gain some of this knowledge. This knowing is, so to speak, a beating around the bush—but it beats around just *there!* in *that* place! Attempting to know in this way does not result from our natural pride; it radiates from a supernatural humility, if we abide in such a posture. It is the temperate attitude of those who say *both* "we know little, too little, Lord!" *and* "we have much to learn, there is much to learn here." We cannot help but feel the texture of Torah: to notice that Torah entails something completely different than all pagan, natural religion. We know that with this we are beginning to enter a different spiritual world; we draw near to a new joy.

Let us then examine how we should describe the *unity* of divine virtues, proceeding from the assumption that their unity is actually Love.

5.

God is Love (1 John 4:8). This confession once and for all repudiates all speculation about God as silent *Being*. God is not "eternal" in the sense that we understand with our unsanctified mind. God is not the intellectual *remainder* after we have subtracted all life and movement from the divine self. When we read the Bible and we do not bring such philosophy with us, we find no trace of this thinking, no matter where we open the Bible or how we connect its promises and confessions, narratives and instructions. In point of fact, we have already communicated this truth in our discussion of the Name and its radix, YHWH. This *one* name of God is not a name of human derivation; it indicates the *grondvorm*, ground-form, enclosing the divine Name—and Revelation. It does not signify "the Eternal One"; or the "I am"; or the "I will be"; but rather, "I will *be-there*"; "I will be-there for you"; "I will be with you as I will be with you; you will certainly recognize me!" God's "eternity" consists in God's lordship and guidance of the eons: God accompanies the elect people *le-olam*; in *saecula saeculorum*, from age to age.

God is Love, and from this confession we learn to notice *this* eternity, which, in moving itself, brings forth the movement of ages. We ask ourselves whether it says something to us, perhaps, that the Messiah is called "the Everlasting Father" (Isa 9:6); or that Habakkuk proclaims, "[God's] ways are everlasting" (Hab 3:6). These texts do not justify the claim that immutability is more divine than mutability, or that stasis is more divine than movement, or that spirit is more divine than nature. We cannot maintain such ideas if we have learned anything from the biblical ABCS, nor if we have learned to spell that God is Love.

God is Love, and therefore, God's way of being cannot be distinguished from that of creation on the basis of *categories* like stasis and movement, being and becoming, spirit and nature, visible and invisible, immutable and mutable. God is motionless *and* in motion; in God both being *and* becoming become visible, spirit *and* nature are found. God is both visible *and* invisible, immutable *and* mutable.

Statements like that are not, rightly understood, abstract truths. To the contrary, we renounce autonomous abstractions (we know that philosophy remains but a solitary projection from solitary reflection). We seek to honor *the Name*: to dwell in the world of the holy Teaching—and as such, to acknowledge and testify, by means of a detour, from a distance, that God is Love. We never trust in the image—amplified and exaggerated a hundredfold—of our last, emptiest, most abstract idea. Instead we trust the Teaching, which will guide us.

5a.

But how is God to be understood "in Godself"? The answer to this question is: *no differently* from the way God approaches us in God's self-revelation. If in this revelation we encounter an event of Love, then it follows that in God's own self, Love is a continuous event. God's Being is not a static and fixed Being. Rather, God is a *Being-in-Act*. The Bible invites this concept, because in this way we understand the *unity* of what the Bible says about God: on the one hand, God is absolute and perfect—but on the other hand, God "comes"; God "descends"; God "hides." God *wills* to be, and wills to be Godself, and sustains Godself. God's Being is a Being that constitutes itself. Scripture and the dogma speak of *Father, Son, and Spirit*; these three "persons" are *one*, eternal God. We cannot expound this truth any further here. It is enough in this context, while rehearsing the biblical ABCs, to accustom ourselves to— and at the same time, to stay astonished at—God: that the God with whom we have to do is a fullness of life and a *schenkende Tugend,* gift-giving virtue.[1] Nothing is so dissimilar to God as Nature, or at least, the kind of Nature that our science envisions: a series of powers governing all things according to the laws of cause and effect, and which remain eternally the same.

THE LIVING ONE IS GOD

5b.

We now understand somewhat better what we may learn from the *form* of the Bible: namely, it is *narrated*. Narrative follows narrative telling of God's encounter with the elect people and with individual persons. The Bible is meant for proclamation, and it leads us as teaching—but at the same time, it consists of a wild variety of stories, songs, and commandments, without any demonstrable *unity* or overarching structure. These qualities are not a deficiency in comparison with, for instance, the systematic sacred texts of the Indian religion. The *apparently less* is in reality the sign and seal of what is *superior*: the Love of God. That is, the miscellany of the Bible is a sign of God's real and "human" way of being. We mean that the likeness of God is found more *readily* in humankind than in nature; in the spontaneity of the spirit than in the causality of the world; in history than in natural laws; in serendipity than in machine-like operations, in irruption than in automation. God's likeness is seen more readily in the madness of surrender than in the monotony of duty; in the beauty of staying faithful within volatile circumstances than in coldly adhering to a law that is unmoved by what is happening.

Love is not a generic quality, distributed throughout the world like ether or air. No: "love" means that God BECOMES INVOLVED with people to whom God is not obliged, and in *such a way* that God is and remains ungraspable. That God is Love cannot—thanks be to God!—be proven, but it is—praise God!—testified to us. The Bible does not demonstrate it based on God's eternal Being, but it does narrate it to us, again and again. The Bible looks the way it looks because of this. Not just one text gives witness, directly and succinctly, that God is love; and not just one or another narrative shows God's grace and forgiveness. The *form of Scripture itself*, the shape of the holy Teaching, commends this truth to our hearts. We have not yet suffered enough from the enigma of this life, we have not yet bent down enough beneath the muteness of nature, we have not yet groveled enough before the gods of this age, we have not yet experienced enough of the pain of loneliness, we have not experienced the ghostly silence and arctic cold of the so-called universe, if we don't understand *this* as the ABCs of knowledge: the form of the Bible *presupposes* that God is the Love.

6.

If, according to the Bible, it is true that the unity of God's virtues lies in the event of Love, it entails, furthermore, that God is a *Person*. For if love is proclaimed to us, if the Teaching inducts us into this mystery, then we must accustom ourselves to this reversal of the common conception: it is not the human who is a "person" so that we then talk about God *as if* God were a person by a figure of speech or a simile. Such is the nearly ineradicable misunderstanding of pagans and philosophers: that God is created or understood according to our own image and our own likeness. The Bible says—and it belongs to the biblical ABCs—that God created humans according to *God's* image and according to *God's* likeness. To speak about "personification," or figurative language, or simile, means therefore to speak about creatures, not about God. A human being *is* not a person, but a human *becomes* a person: through the fact, or better, the event of God's Love. Being loved and returning love to God make a human into a person-in-becoming. As the elected and betrothed, the human is predestined to be "conformed to the image of the Son" (Rom 8:29). We may for the time being and with some irony comport ourselves as if the human is already "someone," even if they are, more likely, some*thing*: a handful of dust, a bushel of impressions, a tangle of impulses, a border zone of conflicting, half-unknown powers; in short, a thing, a plant, an animal, a plant-like dreamer, an animal-like fighter. To call this one a "person" would be too much honor, and too much speculation! But see: God is *not* a thing, not a substance. God is action, pure act, singular act; self-sufficient life and love and act. Not just one beloved verse gives witness that God is love, but it is in the Bible everywhere, so that we may learn that God is

PERSON

and—in the full sense—God alone.

7.

Not even the wonderful sentence "God is love" can avoid a certain double-meaning, since it lends some accommodation to the tendency of regarding love as a sort of neutral, impersonal force. God is *the One who Loves*. If it wasn't such a mawkish word, we would simply want to say: God is Lover, *the Lover*. For that reason, the Hasidic rabbis were onto something when they ascribed a more special significance to the *Song of Songs* than to all the other books of the Bible. We act foolishly if we regard Origen and Bernard of Clairvaux and our own Hellebroek[2] as oddballs because they heard the love between Christ and his church in the Song of Songs. They did not tire of listening to it and even wrote lengthy books to convey the magnificence of this union to all who would give ear. Yes indeed, this Song of Songs sings about the essence of the Revelation, clear as day and yet mysteriously, too: the inner structure of Song of Songs contributes to the biblical ABCs by depicting both a seeking and creating kind of love as well as a seeking, receiving kind of love. Some say that Song of Songs was "originally" a collection of love songs. This is doubtless true: in the same way that the Name "actually" is a magic charm, and Hebrew *elohim* is a plural that "originally" referred to multiple gods. This does not embarrass us. On the contrary, the sensuality and ardor, the *passion*, the sweetness of these songs assures us that the love of

God is not a general idea, not a universal force of life, but a personal engagement: a personal election; a personal loyalty. The Gospel of John articulates the loftiest and final word about God as the One who Loves, but even these verses might be understood as too pale or formal, if we did not discern that they are soaked in the ardor and passion of the Song of Songs. Above all, the hidden history *in* history, which is the history of God's people, vaporizes into some pious thoughts, or a precious incident, unless this passion of God sings to our hearts. The holy history is a history of love.

This drama—which in the end amounts to an idyll—is the drama of God's acts and God's struggle to liberate the elect people, God's human children, from the gods; from fear and loneliness. It is the drama of God's initiative to call humankind into the communion of divine love: to meet them, bless them, delight them, and test them. Such drama summarizes the holy history. Song of Songs stands next to the narratives of God encountering Israel—next to them, but apart: it nevertheless recounts the same theme, only in an intensified form. Everything that characterizes human love—one-sided tenacity, eagerness and jealousy, the sorrow of parting, the overcoming of obstacles—all of this is only a distorted silhouette of what is, in God's love, real: of what happens in the holy history.

7b.

Psalms 105, 106, and 107, but also Stephen's speech (Acts 7) and various parables (like the parable of the tenants in Matt 21:3; Mark 12:1; Luke 20:9) give a birds-eye glimpse of the holy history, in that they testify: *God is at work*, because God is the living One, the One who loves, the sovereign lover, the burning and enduring personal presence, the Seeking One, the Acting One, the Leader, the Lover. In the final analysis, the narratives of the exodus from Egypt, the giving of the Law, the exile and return, the sending of prophets, and the advent of the Son recount nothing other than this.

> Set me as a seal upon your heart,
>   as a seal upon your arm;
> for love is *strong as death*,
>   passion fierce as the grave.
> Its flashes are flashes of fire,
>   a raging flame.
> Many waters cannot quench love,
>   neither can floods drown it.
> If one offered for love
>   all the wealth of one's house,
>   it would be utterly scorned (Song of Songs 8:6–7).

Or hear this holy narrative, Ezek 16:4–15:

> As for your birth (Israel), on the day you were born your navel cord was not cut, nor were you washed with water to cleanse you, nor rubbed with salt, nor wrapped in cloths. No eye pitied you, to do any of these things for you out of compassion for you; but you were thrown out in the open field, for you were abhorred on the day you were born. *I passed by you, and saw you* flailing about in your blood. *As you lay in your blood, I said to you, "Live!* and grow up like a plant of the field." You grew up and became tall and arrived at full womanhood; your breasts were formed, and your hair had grown; yet you were naked and bare. I passed by you again and looked on you; you were at the age for love. I spread the edge of my cloak over you, and covered your nakedness: I pledged myself to you and entered into a covenant with you, says the Lord God, and you became mine. Then I bathed you with water and washed off the blood from you, and anointed you with oil. I clothed you with embroidered cloth and with sandals of fine leather; I bound you in fine linen and covered you with rich fabric. I adorned you with ornaments: I put bracelets on your arms, a chain on your neck, a ring on your nose, earrings in your ears, and a beautiful crown upon your head. You were adorned with gold and silver, while your clothing was of fine linen, rich fabric, and embroidered cloth. You had choice flour and honey and oil for food. You grew exceedingly beautiful, fit to be a queen. Your fame spread among the nations on account of your beauty, for it was perfect because of my *splendor* that I had *bestowed* on you, says the Lord God. But you trusted in your beauty, and played the whore because of your fame, and lavished your whorings on any passer-by.

This, too, wants to be nothing other than a summary of the drama of the holy history, in which the love of God was and is *Ereignis*—event.

8.

The *unity* of God's attributes, which is Love, is the miracle par excellence. The miracle does not consist in God's remaining an unthinkable unity—an absolute and perfect self-identity—within the plurality of divine virtues: living, personal, loving. Rather, *this* is the *miracle* proclaimed to us: that *God*'s faithfulness and *our* unfaithfulness are *together* and stay together. It is not in God's majesty *above* the contradictions of our lives and thoughts, but in God's majesty despite and *in the midst of* our contradictions. God is *God* amidst our turning away and turning toward, our searching and losing, our praise and contempt. These contradictions reveal the divinity of God, the oneness and uniqueness of God, as *God's love*.

If we say that God is a Person, this claim is only an *inference* from the word narrated by the holy history: namely, that God is the One who Loves. In the same way that the point of the section on the Name of God is not just that one God exists, but that *this* God is God, in this context, it is not a theoretical point that God is Person, but it signifies that God is Love in the *unity* of divine virtues, or, even better: that God is the One who Loves.

Proclamation is a joyful announcement of a joyful event. It belongs as such —and let us not forget this—to the *instruction*; and instruction according to our definition, "takes place under the saving power of the One who alone knows what is right, who alone has the right to render judgment, and who alone is able to give right direction to our lives."[3] All of this, and in particular this doctrine of the *unity* of divine virtues, aims to make us feel more at home with the Bible, and to initiate us into *simchat torah*, the *joy of the teaching*, in abiding wonder at the knowledge of God: of *this* God, who is Love.

8a.

Such joy can snatch a church, a people, a human being, from the edge, or even from the abyss of

NIHILISM,

which is the intention to live from out of bare life and to act purely for the sake of acting. This ethos amounts to untethered thinking and aimless action. We cannot create norms and ideals whenever we need them. They are powerless against the wild emptiness that precipitated them, against our modern soul, weakened by anger and petty games. That emptiness hides in our hearts, which have become newly respectable, ordinary, and sterile because of prosperity. After all, nothing is more truly *nihil*, nothing, than mediocrity, which raises no question or bitterness. Nihilistic barbarity seems worse to us, since it concerns us more physically. But it has a certain grandeur in comparison to the streamlined masses such as Aldous Huxley's *Brave New World* depicts. It will be clear to us that even the new *paganism*—that compulsive attempt to worship Life, Fate, the State, the Hero again in a godless universe—that even this neo-mystical paganism will be devoured by the sterile nihilism of cravens and pleasure-seekers. There seems to be no stopping it.

Such nothingness is not nothing, but rather: rebellion. Its true character enters the light fully where Love has appeared, which is and remains our situation *after* Christ. God's virtues find their unspeakable *unity* in Love, *this* Love. It is free, it is powerful, and it is sovereign. The futility of nihilistic rebellion thereby becomes clear. Through the power of this Love, rebellion is shown to be powerless, moribund, a dead-end.

Why do the nations conspire,
    and the peoples plot *in vain*?
The kings of the earth set themselves,
    and the rulers take counsel together,
    against the Lord and his anointed (Ps 2:1–2).

And we know that the Son of God has come and has given us understanding so that we may know him who is the Truthful One; and we are in him who is true, in his Son Jesus Christ. He is the true God and eternal life. Little children, keep yourselves from idols (1 John 5:20–21, NRSV adapt.).

But how can we do this, keeping ourselves from idols, except by dwelling in the holy Teaching and experiencing the abiding joy of Torah? At the last, nothing counters Nothingness but Love, *this* Love. "It bears all things, believes all things, hopes all things, endures all things. Love never ends" (1 Cor 13:7, 8a). Therefore: all in-between measures are crushed by the violence of this decision:

Either Love, *this Love*—

or Nothingness, the barbaric *or* the bourgeois nihilism of "God is dead."

We can now understand why John didn't just consider denial of the *incarnation* of God as a different religion or a heresy, but as "the spirit of the antichrist, of which you have heard that it is coming; and now it is already in the world" (1 John 4:3). If Love were merely an attribute of God, then it would perhaps be possible to dispute this point, but now that love is the *unity* of virtues, and the Event *itself*, the Revelation *itself*, the Salvation *itself*, it follows that rejecting love indicates the grand and futile *anti!* and the nullification of the meaning of life.

NOTES

1. Miskotte quotes Friedrich W. Nietzsche, *Also sprach Zarathustra*, KSA 4 (Berlin: de Gruyter, 1988), who dedicates a section to "Von der schenkende Tugend" (97–102).

2. Abraham Hellebroek (1658–1731) was a Dutch minister who authored an influential collection of sermons on the mystical reading of the Song of Songs. His work was read in Miskotte's time and continues to be read today among pietistic Reformed Christians in the Netherlands.

3. See chapter 2, paragraph 8 (p. 11).

Chapter 7

The Acts

1.

No other power obscures the holy Teaching more than the capacity for *thinking things through*. In itself—it hardly needs saying—this ability is a good gift, indispensable to common people and a sign of their human dignity. Thinking through the consequences of simple or simple-looking slogans, both according to their origins in human rebellion and their results for human society, is a task that is, regrettably, seldom taken up. This in spite of our tradition of spiritual level-headedness and the extraordinary state of our education, which might provide reason for the opposite, more optimistic expectation.

However, where "God" is concerned, we can arrive only at Nothingness if we think things through according to our own ways; it is imperative we let ourselves be determined and limited by the Name. And, as far as the attributes of God are concerned, we are bound to arrive at Fate, if we attempt to think through the word "Omnipotence" (for example) in our own way. We must be guided and instructed by the order in which Holy Scripture places God's virtues. *When thinking things through, we are bound to an unchanging rule.*

And yet everything can still be distorted. Those virtues themselves can be *distorted* into monsters and monstrous masks, into puppets and idols of our religious fantasy, when we would understand virtues such as righteousness, wisdom, or patience as self-contained qualities; as character traits of a god, a god-picture. Reason and level-headedness are no help against this evil possibility, since they break down under duress, and so become embarrassed and confused, in the head and on paper and as a way of life. The only help against this possibility is the holy Teaching, which instructs us beforehand concerning the act-character of God's revelation:

the ACT-CHARACTER,

namely, the revelation of God's virtues, which interrupts our way of thinking, and possibly even prevents our wandering away into error in the first place.

1a.

We want to learn afresh to read Scripture with each other: to hear and experience and proclaim it as *teaching*—about the Name and the virtues of God. We should not wonder that this is necessary in every time, and especially during times of upheaval. *Rather* it should *amaze* us that even though many people come into contact with the results of this new reading—whether through written texts, or preaching, or lectures and testimonies—and then, regardless their disposition toward Scripture, warm-hearted or critical, *they default back* to "correct" and "dogmatic" words and ideas. In olden days, such words and ideas helped to organize and educate Christians, and for those old-time Christians, who know how to translate them, they still convey important truths. But these antique concepts have become *antiquated* because of their received form. Their obsolescence is not a matter of truth (for they were never in a strong sense the truth), but of their capacity to serve as instruments: as vehicles to a closer understanding of the truth. Some will say that a new dogmatic theology is needed. And indeed that is correct, and, thanks be to God, a foundation for that work is already laid in our time. But as a congregation, as a people, as captives of the current time, we cannot yet attend to that, we are not able to, and nor do we need it yet, so long as we discard the old dogmatic terms, or cast them in the crucible, and make ourselves more *childlike* and receptive to the Teaching, that is, the continual instruction of Scripture, including, first of all, its *grondstructuur* or ground-structure, its method, its language, the sound of its speech, the unity of its witness.

This does not mean that we have become biblicists, that is, people who believe they can proclaim the fullness of the Word without reference to church and dogma. We concede that this is not possible, because it would result in new, one-sided, and self-sufficient interpretations. On the other hand, no one would deny that Holy Scripture can be accessed quite without the "support" of interpretive devices such as "biblical infallibility." At the same time, only the strangers in Jerusalem, alienated from contemporary society, will deny that tenets such as that have become a hindrance for thousands and thousands.

In order to avoid one-sidedness, the following should also be noted.

It is necessary to let the Bible itself speak again in its own language—and to let the Bible *finish speaking*. We must renounce the tradition of reading short pericopes; we should rethink our beloved texts as well our texts of terror. Perhaps it would benefit us to experience shock again at the Bible's original color and impact. Many nowadays (e.g., in preaching) are voicing these raw accents again, in order to let the Bible speak, and so to break the spell of its dignified silence; to cut loose the ribbon on the decorative bouquet that the Bible has become. Some will say at this point: such an approach reveals the Bible's actual bloodiness—it is anything but an edifying story! Violence, lust, and passion reign within it. The prophet becomes a whirling dervish, the spirit of the Lord descends in a frenzy. The parables of Jesus feature grifters, scoundrels, and lowlifes. What is senseless and abhorrent in Scripture does come into view. In such a situation, we understand the desperate urge to flee the (awful) and pious atmosphere of conventional "Bible studies." There is nothing wrong with that urge—so long as we hold fast to the *unity* of Scripture in spite of its kaleidoscopic variety; so long as we observe the order of God's virtues in spite of their wild abundance; so long as we keep before our eyes the direction and climax of God's acts in spite of their arbitrariness. In other words: we must get off the promenade of doctrine—but so, too, must we desist from the Charleston dance of biblicism. Neither felt slippers nor (very artistic!) clogs will do us any good.

Will we then become boring again? I don't believe so, if we succeed with our synthesis—or better: if it is given to us to see *why* in the first place we had to shatter the numb fixity of our system with the raw materials of the Bible itself. We did not pursue this breakthrough just to be able to speak in new, interesting accents, but rather to know *God*, as *God has given the divine self to be known*; to distinguish God from conceptual ideas about God. Thinking things through, listing out consequences and totalling them up, threatens the true Teaching—just as taking isolated biblical persons and events threatens to obscure the Teaching on the other side. In the meantime, in more or less churchly circles, the danger of thinking things through on our own looms large. In these circles, nothing is more current than the theme that we have now addressed in this chapter.

2.

All these disputed assumptions obscure *this* moment that takes place in the form of the biblical witness: *God's acts determine our knowledge of God's virtues.* This moment has been so deeply impoverished or hidden, made invisible to the people of our generation, that even our decision to speak about divine righteous*ness*, loving-kind*ness,* and the other virtues in the abstract can appear questionable. We forget all too easily the origin and legitimating basis of these abstract words; for they are founded nowhere else than in the act, which God, *this* God, has wrought upon the earth, and sets before our eyes, and commissions us to tell by word of mouth and from one generation to the next. The attributes of God are the *attributes of God's actions*. What we say about God, what comes to our lips in praise and prayer, can be nothing else than an inference from God's *actions*, from *God*'s deeds. For reading the Bible and for practicing a life guided by the holy Teaching, everything depends on the act-character of God's revelation. The accusation that this doctrine is anemic is misplaced, in that we have clarified every theoretical reflection is abstract and anemic, whether on nature, on history, or any other aspect of reality. The right to accuse lies in fact with those who desire, with reference to God, to encounter the reality itself, and to keep engaged with that reality. To this extent, although we think that much of the haranguing against dogmatism is stupid and blindness, we must stand in solidarity with our fellow humans who have been touched by this desire to experience reality itself.

3.

As we awaken from the slumber of our theories, we need to discern that God's Act is

PRIMARY.

Such is the manifest intention of the whole Counsel that governs human life and all the parameters of reality wherein we dwell. Take note of the Sabbath Psalm (92):

> It is good to give thanks to the Lord,
>   to sing praises to your *Name*, O Most High;
> to declare your steadfast love in the morning,
>   and your faithful*ness* by night,
> For you, O Lord, have made me glad by your *work*;
>   at the *works* of your hands I sing for joy.

Notice the sense of anticipation among the multitude when they hear the ecstatic voices of the disciples at the Feast of Pentecost (Acts 2:7–8, 11b):

> Amazed and astonished, they asked, "Are not all these who are speaking Galileans? And how is it that we hear, each of us, in our own native language . . . in our own languages we hear them speaking *about God's deeds of power.*"

And hear how this language is employed throughout Scripture:

Come, behold the works of the Lord (Ps 46:8).

And I say, "It is my grief
  that the right hand of the Most High has changed."
I will call to mind the deeds of the Lord;
  I will remember your wonders of old.
I will meditate on all your work,
  and muse on your mighty deeds (Ps 72:10–12).

He made known his ways to Moses,
  his acts to the people of Israel (Ps 103:7).

They forgot what he had done,
  and the miracles that he had shown them (Ps 78:11).

The works of his hands are truth (Ps 111:7, NRSV adapt.).

The Rock, his work is perfect (Deut 32:4).

"Believe me that I am in the Father and the Father is in me; but if you do not, then believe me because of the works themselves" (John 14:11).

Look, you scoffers!
  Be amazed and perish,
for in your days I am doing a work,
  a work that you will never believe, even if someone tells you (Acts 13:41).

4.

So then: Creation is an *Act*, and the Covenant is an *Act*, and God's providential guidance is an *Act*; the Exodus from Egypt is an *Act* (with outstretched arm), and the exile is an Act. We should not be concerned first and foremost about the *unity* of these acts, or about their foundation or goal. There is a Counsel of God; there is a Way of God over the earth. We speak about these. But first things first: we are confronted with the *acts* of the Lord; they delimit the space within which the decisive moments of faith take place (or do not take place; or are refused). They create the realm within which people gather to praise the Name. For in these acts, people encounter—better to say, not the righteous*ness* of God, but the *righteous God*: God as God alone is righteous, the one who judges the world, and restores life, and puts humankind in its proper place. They encounter—again, better to say, not the mercifu*lness* of God, but the *merciful God*, or God as God alone is merciful, who sustains the world, and makes life possible, covering over humans with acquittal and forgiveness, joy and peace.

IN THE ACT, GOD'S PRESENCE IS REVEALED

> I shall not die, but I shall live,
>> and recount the *deeds* of the Lord.
> The Lord has punished me severely,
>> but he did not give me over to death.
> Open to me the gates of righteousness,
>> that I may enter through them
>> and give thanks to the Lord.
> This is the gate of the Lord;
>> the righteous shall enter through it (Ps 118:17–20).

See, to say: "to act is a human characteristic, but God is eternally resting"—that would merely exchange one anthropomorphic idea for another one. The second idea here, that God is resting, is simply *wrong*, and insofar as it is possible for a human thought, it destroys salvation. What God's rest means, we need to understand *from* God's acts; the sense of the image "rest" must derive from the sense of the image "act," and not vice versa. This specific understanding belongs to the preparation for a faithful and receptive reading of the Bible, which is both new and classic, and then again, new. Peace is also the fruit of the divine Acts. Do we still hear this, from the very beginning, from Genesis?

> Thus the heavens and the earth were finished, and all their multitude. And on the seventh day God finished the work that he had done, and he rested on the seventh day from all the work that he had done. So, God blessed the seventh day and hallowed it, because on it God rested from all the work that he had done in creation (Gen 2:1–3).

4a.

To speak like this about creation is a consequence of God's act in history. An example can be found in the song that was sung after the passage through the Red Sea (Exodus 15):

> I will sing to the *Lord*, for he has triumphed gloriously;
>> horse and rider he has thrown into the sea.
> The *Lord* is my strength and my might,
>> and he has become my salvation;
> this is my God, and I will praise him,
>> my father's God, and I will exalt him.
> The Lord is a warrior;
>> the Lord is his name.

The enemy said, "I will pursue, I will overtake,
  I will divide the spoil (. . .)
 my hand shall destroy them."
You blew with your wind, the sea covered them;
  they sank like lead in the mighty waters.
"Who is like you, O *Lord*, among the gods?
  Who is like you, majestic in holiness,
  awesome in splendor, doing wonders? (literally: what is torn off, cut off, the impossible)[1]
You stretched out your right hand,
  the earth swallowed them,
until your people, O Lord, passed by,
  until the people whom you acquired passed by.
You brought them in and planted them on the mountain of your own possession,
  the place, O Lord, that you *made* your *abode*.
The Lord will reign forever and ever.

5.

The act-character of Revelation has several consequences for our reading and learning and living. First, *not everything that happens can be regarded as an "act of God."* If that were the case, we would be cast back onto the naked existence of things and the naked facts. If everything that happens were an act of God, we would never be able to praise God on account of the contradictions of our experience. Or we would have to screw ourselves up from faith to sight, and so gain the perspective of angels and archangels! If this were so, the divine virtues would be drowned out by grim Omnipotence, which does not govern, but simply *is*, in the same way that nature is: then we would have to erase the Name again and *either* sink down into a nameless void *or* be driven back into the arms of the so-called gods.

If everything that happens were an act of God, then spiritual life in a biblical sense would fade away to a "pagan" reverence before so-called Providence; spiritual judgment would be violated by mute facticity; praise in the community would perish. If narrating, praising, and celebrating the acts of the Lord are not undertaken with *attentiveness to the particular*, the exceptional, the whole liturgy and worship of God is robbed of meaning. It is not enough for the act of God to be only *exceptional*, since Satan also does his share of exceptional deeds, according to the manner and chaotic style of his reign. The exceptional character of God's acts consists in their performance *in* the world and yet also *against* the downward spiral of history. This contrasts with the actions of the demons, which, for all their exceptionality, are done *in* the world and *for* the world; they confirm the world in its absurdity and alienation, unto hardening.

6.

Therefore, with reference to the acts of the Lord, we are given a *criterion*: one central act that is singular and unique, final and unreserved (though preceded and followed by related acts, wonders, and signs). This *one* act is

the SENDING of the SON,

the coming of the Messiah, the totality of his words, works, and wonders, the act-of-all-acts, which is his death and resurrection. There and there alone we may learn the character, the meaning, and the goal of all the acts that God has done *in* the world and yet *against* the world. And now we may add: *on behalf of* the world.

If we *believe* in Jesus Christ, we not only accept that such a miraculous, god-human person existed or still exists in some mystical way. We do not finally put our trust in God by virtue of a *fact* that took place, or a situation that has since come into being. We *believe*: meaning that we *ac*tually enter, with the act of our life, into the Act of God. Such a thing is possible, because the word and the deed appear to us here in complete unity, and do not remain more or less separated from each other as in other cases. In the revelation of Jesus Christ, that is, we *embrace* the Word, the Act, the *unity* of the virtues, the Name, the Presence of God in this world and in our lives.

It is not the role of an introductory and preparatory work like this one to discuss this central miracle, which governs both the times preceding it and following it. That miracle belongs to proclamation, and to reflection on proclamation, which is called dogmatics: dogmatics conceived as guidance for preaching. We cannot completely avoid the Bible's principal content—it is the Bible's very purpose to attest it! Indeed we always maintain contact with the Bible's intention and goal by holding as much as possible before our eyes the ABCs: in the formal sense, understood as an elementary grammar (i.e., the *language* and *speech* through which Scripture differentiates itself from a book, also and especially from other "sacred writings"). It suffices for now to assert this: the *criterion* of the acts of God, about which we read in Scripture, is shown to us in the sending of the Son.

6a.

This criterion and this focus make it clear to us how much—both *before* and *after* the coming of the Son—the life of humankind depends on *encounter* with the God who is the One who sent Christ. At the same time, *this* sequence becomes clear: first the Old, then the New Testament, and finally the Old again. Encounters *before* and *after* Christ are in essence encounters with the same God, YHWH. The Bible does not yield up a closed system, and yet it forms a unity deriving from a theme that is true both before and after Christ: the acts of the Lord become encounters for us. On account of this, the Teaching is a "world to dwell in": it speaks about our own life. We still have no better songs than the psalms; the essence of affliction and abandonment is nowhere expressed better than in the books of Lamentations and Job. The same holds true for the narratives. Because they narrate encounter with God (the God who remains the same), they are teaching and promise for us and for every day. Where else will we learn that *spiritual life is ordinary life, that it is blessed with encounters*—with the acts of God, where God meets us and we meet God's virtues—if not in the so-called Old Testament? For religion, in particular the *zweite Religiosität* or Second Religiousness, which is a more or less artificially induced inwardness, has become isolated these days, just like, for example, the arts.[2]

Living a godly life happens by receiving life through encounter; grieving our distance from God and waiting for the acts of the Lord. The Holy One pervades history. And history is also in every instant *our* history. We learn this by the narratives of encounter, which ring equally true after Christ as they did before Christ. The mysterious aspect is that we learn *from* our focus on the Son to read the Old Testament *in its entire breadth* as a multitude of actions that are summarized in him, and which we now understand by virtue of his appearance as intended *for us also*; "all scripture is inspired by God and is useful for teaching, for reproof, for correction, and for training in righteousness" (2 Tim 3:16).

7.

The focus of this chapter, which seems to contract our field of vision, leads to the reverse: namely, to a *broadening* of our perception of the "acts of the Lord," to world-historical and even cosmic dimensions. The ABCs, the *grondvorm* or ground-form of the Bible, pressed us to reject the naive or speculative assumption that everything naturally belongs to God and originates from God. But this truth now receives its rightful place according to the structure governing our interpretation.

We said: Creation is *act*, the Covenant is *act*, Providence is *act*, and others—we do not take anything back. On the contrary, we can now *break through* the initial restraint that we observed, in order forcefully and emphatically to praise Creation and Covenant and Providence. For we have learned from the holy Teaching to praise these acts for the sake of the Messiah and the "footsteps of God's anointed" (Ps 89:51), whether in his first or second coming. These acts reflect, announce, prepare, or unfold *the* Act.

After all, it is not the case that outside the Torah, the world is haunted with riddles from which we must avert our eyes, lest they eclipse our salvation;

it is far from the case that the sacred Teaching guides us by bypassing the raw reality of life; the gospel is not a lonely word of consolation, standing desolately within an abandoned world and forsaken human hearts. On the contrary, the Torah wants to reveal the mystery of the single Act as the witness concerning God, the Father, the Almighty!

For in him all the fullness of God was pleased to dwell, and through him God was pleased to reconcile all things to the divine self, whether on earth or in heaven, by making peace through the blood of his cross (Col 1:19). For in him all things in heaven and on earth were created, things visible and invisible, whether thrones or dominions or rulers or powers—all things have been created through him and for him (Col 1:16).

The last things can be spoken of only in visions. This is how they are recorded in the prophets and in the Apocalypse, the revelation to John. There and there precisely we hear again about the battle, the heavenly battlefield, the true history, in which Michael and his armies challenge Satan and his deputies to a decisive battle for the world. God acts: God, who was, and is, and is to come.

"Let us rejoice and exult and give him the glory" (Rev 19:7), because the Lord, the Almighty God, has established royal deeds.[3]

Admittedly it is the case that Scripture knows about the *silence* of God; it is noteworthy that this silence indicates an absence of acting rather than an absence of speaking.

"Is it not the case that you don't fear me, because I am silent? (Isa 57:11)"[4]—"These things you have done and I have been silent" (Ps 50:21)—"For Zion's sake I will not keep silent, and for Jerusalem's sake I will not rest, until her vindication shines out like the dawn, and her salvation like a burning torch" (Ps 50:3; Isa 65:6; 62:1).

The immense weight of Silence indicates from afar the magnitude of the immense glory of the royal acts concerning the End.

NOTES

1. The parentheses are Miskotte's own clarificatory gloss.

2. Miskotte borrows the concept of *zweite Religiosität* or Second Religiousness from Oswald Spengler, *The Decline of the West, Volume* I, trans. Charles Francis Atkinson (Alfred A Knopf, 1926 [German original 1918]), 424.

3. Miskotte gives the impression that the second part of this sentence is part of the quotation from Revelation, but it is not.

4. Miskotte provides his own paraphrase of the Isaiah text.

Chapter 8

Word

1.

The phrase that occurs more often than any other in Scripture, so often that we might gloss over it out of habit and boredom, is this: *"And God said."* "Then God spoke." Already this claim distinguishes the creation story, for example, from the seemingly similar mythologies of the nations. "Then God said, 'Let there be light'; and there was light" (Gen 1:3).

In paganism, people speak or shout to silent Fate. The deeper this silence becomes, the more shrilly do human cries ring out, until they are stifled, and they ebb into the cruel silence of submission, which amounts to the *death* of the soul.

YHWH speaks! *Thus* says the Lord—

One can relate this feature of the ABCs to the common Eastern outlook that assigns "magical," conjuring, and enchanting power to the word—but one might then forget to observe what is specific to Israel. There, if one wants to speak of magic, such magical power is attributed to *God* and to the word of *God*. "In the beginning was the Word, and the Word was with God, and the Word was God. All things came into being through him, and without him not one thing came into being" (John 1:1, 3). Some find in that a confirmation of their own abstract philosophy, as, for example, Fichte,[1] while others experience Israel's point of view as foreign and grumble like Spengler against a magical worldview and "Arabic culture."[2]

In the end, our treatment of the biblical ABCs need not engage this question about the spiritual language of Scripture as a whole, and it can turn instead to the linguistic expressions themselves. The Bible is about what God said then-and-then, there-and-there, but always on earth and to humans. Hold this before your eyes: God's speech does not begin with the genesis of the world, but it begins to dawn in human lives. It dawns within the soul, and then the light shines everywhere. "Within the soul"—no, that does not sound biblical enough, the expression is too detached, too otherworldly, too dim. The Word comes to *humans*, in the totality of their existence, as an event. "The Lord sent a word against Jacob, and it fell on Israel" (Isa 9:8), like a stone, a meteor, a seed.

2.

In the same way that the act of God is an act of salvation and generates history, holy history, so also is God's word *a saving word.*

In the same way that Israel's knowledge of God can be traced back from the act of Deliverance to the Creation-as-Act, so also does knowledge of God's word of revelation extend back, deductively, to the word of creation. The Lord spoke to humankind, to Abraham, to the prophets, and that brought about salvation and unlocked a peaceful kingdom and sealed the significance of the chosen life. *From out of this point*, the prophetic spirit must understand that creation originates from the same source: the Word. God *said*: You are mine (Isa 43:1). Because God said this, I know that God also *said*: Let there be light.

Creation is salvation insofar as it serves the salvation of souls. Creation has given salvation, which is the triumph of the Lord, an ever-renewing ground and basis in the eternal future.

The Word is *spoken* word, a voice calling on another who is spoken *to*. For this reason, the *dative*, the third case, occurs frequently throughout Scripture, but in particular in receipt of the Word. The dative case expresses giving, communicating, seeking community and, as the complement on the human side, thanksgiving, surrendering, endeavoring.[3] The essence of creation does not obtain within creation itself, but in its relationship to the One who sustains creation through the Word.

3.

But God called to Adam, and said to him, "where are you?" (Gen 3:9)

Then God spoke all these words: I am the Lord your God, who brought you out of the land of Egypt, out of the house of slavery (Exod 20:1).

In God, whose word I praise,
    in the Lord, whose word I praise (Ps 56:10).

Long ago God spoke to our ancestors in many and various ways by the prophets, but in these last days he has spoken to us by a Son (Heb 1:1–2a).

All people are grass,
   their constancy is like the flower of the field.
The grass withers, the flower fades;
   but the word of our God will stand for ever (Isa 40:6b, 8a).

You have already been cleansed by the word that I have spoken to you (John 15:3).

One does not live by bread alone,
but by every word that comes from the mouth of God (Deut 8:3; Matt 4:4).

The time is surely coming, says the Lord God,
   when I will send a famine on the land;
not a famine of bread, or a thirst for water,
   but of hearing the *words* of the Lord.
They shall wander from sea to sea,
   and from north to east;
they shall run to and fro, seeking the word of the Lord,
   but they shall not find it (Amos 8:11, 12).

I *tell* you this now, before it occurs, so that when it does occur, you may believe that I am he (John 13:19).

The one who rejects me and does not receive my word has a judge; on the last day the word that I have spoken will serve as judge (John 12:48)

And *from there* the testimony shines throughout the space of the world: regarding the One "who sustains *all things* by his powerful word" (Heb 1:3).

Of the coming Messiah, it says: "with the breath of his lips he shall kill the wicked" (Isa 11:4b).

By the word of the Lord the *heavens* were made,
    and all their host by the breath of his mouth (Ps 33:6).

In the beginning was the Word (John 1:1)

Then he said to me, "It is done!" (Rev 21:6)

And between these two, in the middle of time: "I have heard that the Messiah is coming, and when he comes, he will proclaim all things to us." Jesus said to her, *"I am he, the one who is speaking with you"* (John 4:25b–26, NRSV, adapt.).

This attentiveness to the Word characterizes the entirety of Scripture so insistently that it must shake us awake and stir up in us a presentiment about the meaning of the divine naiveté and the condescension of grace: the word, the word, and again the word, at the beginning and the end and in the middle. And for us,

the middle is decisive.

3a.

If we would heed the language of the Bible, then we can do nothing more beneficial than take notice of the distinctions given in it—without too quickly pressing for unity. If such unity ever appears before our eyes, it will arise *from out of* the Bible's plurality, and at the end of our hearing rather than at the beginning.

We must distinguish the ways that God's act comes to us:

a The word that *calls*, the word of election, for which Abraham is the premier example (Gen 12:1).
b The word that *judges* (which is to say, it separates and sets us right and gives us direction), for which the striking down of Ananias is a clear example (Acts 5:5).
c The word that *heals*, which is a word of power par excellence. A military man once spoke about this with beautiful restraint: "only speak the word, and my servant will be healed. For I also am a man under authority, with soldiers under me; and I say to one, 'Go,' and he goes, and to another, 'Come,' and he comes, and to my slave, 'Do this,' and the slave does it" (Matt 8:8b–9).

Though we may hardly know what we are saying, we may name the *unity* of this calling, judging, and healing, the word that *creates*. This word is the effectual going-out of the One "who gives life to the dead and calls into existence the things that do not exist" (Rom 4:17b). It dizzies us to imagine that this creative act is a continuous event, an occurrence that carries and surrounds us and draws us onward to an indescribable future.

Nonetheless, we confuse the spiritual ABCs, tarnishing their clarity and forfeiting their modesty, so necessary for fruitful use of the Bible, if we forget that this creative word never actually presents itself *as creative*. The word that creates does not present itself as a *saving* word unless we proceed from the Name of God and therefore hear this word as *God's* saving word. We need also to keep before us always the *grondvormen*, ground-forms, of "calling," "judging," and "healing," in order concretely to learn their content, and in the right sequence.

See:

a Exod 3:4f; 1 Sam 3:4f; Isa 6:5; Jer 1:6; Hos 11:1; Isa 43:1; Matt 4:19; John 1:43; Rom 1:1; Gal 5:13; Eph 4:4; 1 Tim 6:12; 1 Pet 1:15;
b 1 Sam. 2:6: "The Lord kills and brings to life; he brings down to Sheol and raises up"; Deut 32:39; Jer 22:29; Zech 12:1; Mal 1:1; Hos 4:6; Heb 2:1–3; John 12:48;
c Isa 43:11: "I, I am the Lord, and besides me there is no healer" (NRSV, adapt.); "*Talitha cum*," which means, "Little girl, get up!" (Mark 5:41f); "*Ephphatha*," that is, "Be opened" (Mark 7:34); but also, emphatically: "Friend, your sins are forgiven you" (Luke 5:20), to compare with John 6:63: "The words that I have spoken to you are spirit and life."

"And in the very place where it was said to them, 'You are not my people,' there they shall be *called* children of the living God" (Rom 9:26; Hos 1:10). "For he spoke, and it came to be; he commanded, and it stood firm" (Ps 33:9).

4.

Now for the reverse: what makes human beings human is, according to the holy Teaching, that they have the *word*. They are not lonely within the world; they need not keep company solely with creation, as happens with the making of a work of art. To humans has been given language, the crown of creation, the gateway to all spiritual communion, the window and vista to eternal glory.

Language itself has an exceptional position: chosen and appointed for a *service* that goes beyond all human works. It contains at the same time both the mystical and the transparent, if not also the sobriety of pure logic, which only mathematical logic can topple from its pride of place. Language uncovers the mystery of non-loneliness, of *address as a Thou*, which belongs to the paradisal state. Humans speak because they are spoken to. They answer, they call out—they call *upon* God, *this* God whose Name we spell, whose virtues we know, whose acts we discern in this otherwise so strange and oppressive life. No one knows how long it will take until the mouths of all creation will be opened, and creation will become intelligible as both the Before-World and the Foretelling of the miracle of the end-time. It seems that in the Bible we inhabit this border region and this waiting-time.

Humans stand in the middle of this domain and this time, and *through the gift of the word*, they become involved in the life and purpose of the Lord. Until now we have heard, as is fitting, only about God in these spiritual ABCs. Perhaps we have thought: when will humankind finally enter onto the stage? Well, right *here* is the transition, the first and proper place where humankind receives the calling to and the qualification for human glory and a "humane existence." Listen; humans *speak*, they speak to God or against God or beyond God—in each case, by the power of God's word, they by their own word already have to do with God. No, paganism knows nothing about that; it finds its highest expression in dance, and its most sublime form in heroic silence, bound under Fate. Had not the holy Teaching instructed us and the Spirit overwhelmed our hearts, this speaking would be unknown to us, too.

And now, qualitatively speaking, the response of the beloved is the *true* human word.

Love speaks; the living human utters praise in requital, as an answer to the Name, to Revelation. Revelation is the *love of the Lover*, not of the beloved; but the word, the answer (the prayer, the thanksgiving, and the praise) is the *love of the beloved*. That the Love is particular, that it loves where and when it loves, distinguishes it from the All-Love[4] that merges word and answering word in one.

Love is the stepping-out-of-the-self of that which is hidden. A great mystery is unveiled in the Word *and* the response to it, in prayer and liturgy in general. It seems like only a pious slogan to say that human language is a gift of God. But the claim gains sense and power if we proceed from out of this particular language of love, which is "the Father from whom every family in heaven and on earth takes its name" (Eph 3:15).

4a.

The word is a *saying Yes*, a confirmation, a preservation, a presence and a promise. And the answer to it is a resounding Yes! *Schön*! *Gut*! Amen, that's right, that's how it will be, *Hallelu-yah*, let us praise YHWH for God's calling, judgment, healing, God's creative stepping-out-of-the-self in the entirety of this event. That God is called *good* is the utmost achievement of the human word, if it has undergone the fires of purgation. "O give thanks to the Lord, for *he* is good, for his steadfast love endures forever" (Ps 136:1).

How would the biblical ABCs have benefited us, if we had not delved into the *wonder* of this hidden deep, the realm of the human word? We speak of fatherland and mother tongue, but no human word can find its final meaning unless it discovers the Name as its fatherland and the Word as its native language.

5.

We outline these things *apart from* whether one or another person receives them in faith. This book is a linguistic inventory of the Teaching, the holy instruction; and yet, no matter how formally we approach this topic, or how we position ourselves as outsiders to it, the *decay* of human speech moves us. This threat beleaguers us on many sides during this time. Droves of people cannot leave the holy Teaching without the human word becoming twisted and colorless, because it withdraws from the living relationship of addressing a *Thou*, from the true mystery and paradox, from prayer and praise, witness and parable, and engagement with the neighbor in speech and in writing. In the philosophy that follows just as in the corporate life that follows, the divine miracle of speech dies away. Alienation from God, from *this* God, must result in confusion of speech, mendacity, violence, exaggeration and erosion within this medium of the spirit: in language. One flees into acts that refuse accountability; one flees into feelings and elevates music above the word, in part to circumvent the mystery of one's neighbors; one flees into concepts, abstractions, ciphers, statistics, slogans, catchphrases, abbreviations, rallying cries, shibboleths. Or: one flees into the white magic of artwork, the miracle of singing, the self-contained, perfect word, which is already a turning back toward the way, in intention at least.

5a.

No one should say too quickly: these things do not concern me, because they belong to the ABCs. What is *said* in the world matters to the church. Naturally, the content matters—but also the form and fundament, since everything that happens within the world-of-the-word touches the mission of the church to *lehren* and to *lernen*, to teach and to learn. We know the enormous suggestive power of propaganda, even apart from terror. We now know that language constitutes a people, and that the word of Scripture has constituted the European peoples in their form-of-being.

Only through *living relationship with the Lord of the church can the language of the church become living and life-giving*. Only a perpetual receptivity to the Saving Word, which has gone out into the world in calling, judging, and healing, will be able to keep our reading, learning, and life in the right path. The church has its own vocabulary that its members must actively learn. But it is not for this reason alone that the vicissitudes of language concern the church. The church is not a sect or a club, but a public entity, sent out among the peoples with the word as its medium, its weapon, and its healing balm. Preaching, confessing, praying, dogma and sacramental formulae, singing and teaching, pastoral care, catechizing, glossolalia (speaking in tongues) and ecstatic testimony: they are each eminently a *work* of language. And it is presumption and impudence *not* to consider such works of language as an answer and reflection of the Word of God. As such, they cannot be cleanly distinguished from all the speech that is cultivated in the world or from the dominant streams of discourse in a certain time.

We are very concerned about the extent to which utter nonsense will gain influence—for indeed the rogue word comes crashing down into delirium—and will proclaim, for instance: "might trumps right";[5] "man is a predator"; or to write in verse: "East is East and West is West and never the twain shall meet";[6] or shall teach regarding marriage: "truthfulness trumps faithfulness"—because it is not just illogical and untenable. Such pronouncements reflect a prior and perverse answer to the Word. The human word-world has long been fraying under secret distress: from abuse of the gift of the word and the extinguishing of the brightness of its immanent order.

Whoever hears the Word plunges into the luminous abyss of mystery, but they are certainly torn away from the pool of babbling and vaunting.

6.

What answers have humans given to God's Address?

Cain said, "I do not know; am I my brother's keeper?" (Gen 4:9)

Then they said, "Come, let us build ourselves a city, and a tower with its top in the heavens, and let us make a name for ourselves" (Gen 11:4).

"Let us burst their bonds asunder,
 and cast their cords from us" (Ps 2:3).

And Abraham said, and Moses and the young Samuel: "see, here am I."

Then Mary said, "Here am I, the servant of the Lord; let it be with me according to your word." Then the angel departed from her (Luke 1:38).

The Spirit and the bride *say*, "Come."
 And let everyone who hears say, "Come." Amen. Come, Lord Jesus! (Rev 22:17, 20).

Please take note: this final invitation from Revelation is the last sound heard on this side of the boundary of death; in the same way as the Word of God is a Yes, so, too, is the sincere human word of response a Yes (come!). This is what the Bible calls *faith*, comparable to the story of Mary greeting Elizabeth: "And blessed is she who *believed* that there would be a fulfillment of what was spoken to her by the Lord" (Luke 1:45). The disciples are asked first and foremost: "Who do people say that the Son of Man is? . . . But who do you say that I am?" (Matt 16:13, 15).

Having faith in these examples means *confessing* with heart and *mouth*. Confessing is the primordial act from which deeds of righteousness and love flow forth.

Whoever disturbs this order does not find only a multitude of verses against them, but the *grondstructuur*, ground-structure of Scripture itself rises up against them as if they were a rapist and a destroyer of the mystery of salvation contained in the word; as if they were a profane activist. It is thus impossible that they would be a "doer of the word" (Jas 1:22).

7.

And yet—it is strange, one cannot explain it completely—but the Bible already proclaims in its *grondstructuur* that humankind is called to act, because according to the biblical testimony, God exists in *this* way, as the Name, the virtues, the acts. God speaks in reality, humans answer in reality. Likewise: God's words precede, but the confession of humans comes first, too. God speaks in reality, but in a way that reaches beyond the furthermost reality. In the same way, the faithful speak in reality, but in a way that extends beyond their own miserable reality: *they always say more than they are.* And that is how it should be. Their faith is ahead of their acts; it really cannot be otherwise. "But just as we have the same spirit of faith that is in accordance with scripture—'I believed, and so I spoke'—we also believe, and so we speak" (2 Cor 4:13). The actions follow suit, simply because life itself *consists of actions*—but in the end, it will be just wonderful if we can say, each in our own way: "I have fought the good fight, I have finished the race, I have *kept the faith*" (2 Tim 4:7). It is evidently the most amazing achievement to keep the faith and to keep confirming and confessing it in the midst of the violence we encounter. Truly, in this steadfastness, the human word bears the likeness of the eternal, inviolable Word of God.

NOTES

1. Johann Gottlieb Fichte (1792–1814), in his "On the Ground of Our Belief in a Divine World-Governance," in *J.G. Fichte and the Atheism Dispute (1798–1800)*, ed. Yolanda Estes and Curtis Bowman (London: Ashgate, 2010), 17–30.

2. Oswald Spengler, *The Decline of the West.*

3. Miskotte's passage recalls Franz Rosenzweig: "The dative is . . . the form of belonging, giving, thanking, of submission as well as striving. In it object and subject

come together" (*The Star of Redemption*, trans. William W. Hallo [Notre Dame, IN: Notre Dame University Press, 1970], 129).

4. Miskotte refers here to the All-Love as conceptualized in the anthroposophical teachings of Rudolf Steiner (1861–1925).

5. "Might trumps right" is a phrase that first described the politics of Prussian prime minister Otto von Bismarck (1815–1898).

6. The line occurs in the first and final strophe of Rudyard Kipling's (1865–1936) "The Ballad of East and West" (1889).

Chapter 9

Way

1.

How do the acts and the word of God relate? They are indivisible. The word precedes, and the act illustrates the word. Or again: the act precedes, and the word illuminates the act. The acts of God are *included* in the proclamation of God's virtues (in promise and prophecy; declaration and admonition). If one asks whether there is a complete balance in the ABCs, the answer must be no; the word that *precedes* decisively *outweighs* the word that follows after. Promise is more decisive than admonition: promise does not lose its force even when that which is foretold has come. Preaching that is prophecy does not reach out to comfort only those who live in expectation, before the incursion of the divine act. "I tell you this now, before it occurs, so that when it does occur, you may believe *that I am he*" (John 13:19). It is crucial to believe God, *this* God, on God's *word*. It is likewise crucial that we "follow the example of faith that our ancestor Abraham had" (Rom 4:12), even though the fulfilment of his expectation has come. We must not discard the "signs" that supported faith in his life. This insight about the idiom of faith holds true, accompanied by a good sense for the language, as it were: we do not believe in the acts of the Lord, but in the Word; and we believe in the acts as they are proclaimed to us by the Word.

2.

In the meantime, this description applies to the relationship of God's Word and God's acts *for us*, according to the way we understand them, including and especially in our personal, spiritual life. The Bible, however, contains an *oerwoord*, primordial word, a *grondterm* or ground-term. It usually receives scarce attention, though it expresses something characteristic of the holy Teaching, and it and underlines the Teaching's anti-pagan quality. We mean the word: *Way*. The way of God, or the ways of God—Scripture speaks of these with such emphasis and such relish because in them, the unity of fact and significance, word and deed, promise and fulfillment and then again promise, come fully to light. The Way indicates the *unity* of God's act-as-word and God's word-as-act. We can also put it this way: through this verbal sign, "the Way of God," the mystery of salvation becomes *history*, and history points to the mystery of salvation. Knowledge of God always includes: trust in God's ways. Or, said better: only through knowledge of God's ways do we come to knowledge of the living God.

3.

An inextinguishable idea lives in us humans: since evil can only be conceptualized as the negation of the good, we think that, no matter how briefly, the good ruled on earth for an "eternal" moment. It was at that time the way of humankind began, "the way of all flesh." Is this way encircled only by a motionless Being that lets everything run its course? Or does God also partake in our suffering, in the way of our existence, and the *time* that we live through? Paganism, especially when sublimated to a philosophical worldview, must ignore this question. It must teach that in the beginning, there was chaos! Good and evil, life and death, are entangled from the beginning, rankly and equally entwined. From out of evil springs good, and from out of death, life, and also vice versa, neither has precedence relative to the other. We, who would be instructed by the holy Teaching and who wish to learn the biblical spelling, must say: no, that cannot be true, as surely as the *Lord* is God.

What is real precedes the unreal, what is true *precedes* that which is wrong, justice *before* injustice, life *before* death, not only in an eternal sense, but also in *chronological order*. This mathematical line is so narrow, so thin, almost nonexistent, that we cannot retrieve it. The reality that such things as truth and justice exist—we can know it solely from and through and in the Name, which is to say, Revelation. And *when* we have come to know this, the desire ignites in us for the timeless reign of peace. If we remain in our current state and drink *the cup of time* obediently, we do it because we hear God's word in time. We see God's act and God's sign in time. Above all, though, we learn to understand something of the way of God. What we contemplate as "history" seems to be a breaking of waves, an aimless blowing of wind, a writing of the weightiest things in *sand*; even if they are written with blood, they will still be erased. *After* a bit of reality follows a sea of lies;

after a twilight of justice, a chaos of iniquity; *after* all of life and culture and dreaming, death. What does it profit us, then, to recognize that truth precedes wrong, if it is only an insight of logic? When evil endures, breathing the longest breath in chronological time, and celebrating the rule: "He who laughs last, laughs best"? *And with that, we are so terribly alone!* Because only *we* have history, not the animals nor the angels. Only where there is a beginning and an end can something happen that can be called history. The Word falls here or there, the acts of God take place punctiliarly, there and then. But what about the interstices? *We* ourselves live and suffer in the interstitial places—letting more than leading, undergoing more than overcoming. We dwell in the land of *tohu wa-bohu* [Hebrew for "formless void"], full of dark possibilities. Are the acts of God separated from one other like pointillism? Does there appear only here and there and over yonder a word of God on the earth? Or do the instances connect with each other, do they have an orbit and a goal that we can discern to comfort us? The animals and angels have no history,

> *but God has a history.*

And the humans who know it need never be lonely, not even if the godless laugh. Not even if all of them laughed together, nor if their laughter was the last and best thing we experience.

4.

And so we learn to spell this word in the holy Teaching: *the Way.*

Your way, O God, is in the sanctuary (Ps 77:13a, NRSV adapt.).
Give me life in your way (Ps 119:37b, NRSV adapt.).
The Lord created me (Wisdom) at the beginning of his way (Prov 8:22a, NRSV adapt.).
This God—his way is perfect (2 Sam 22:31a).
In the way of your judgements,
    O Lord, we wait for you (Isa 26:8, NRSV adapt.).

Your ways [are not] my ways, says the Lord.
For as the heavens are higher than the earth,
    so are my ways higher than your ways
    and my thoughts than your thoughts (Isa 55:8b–9).

In the wilderness prepare the way of the Lord,
    make straight in the desert a highway for our God (Isa 40:3).

God's way is in whirlwind and storm,
   and the clouds are the dust of his feet.
He rebukes the sea . . . The mountains quake before him,
   and the hills melt;
the earth heaves before him,
   the world and all who live in it (Nah 1:3b–5, NRSV adapt.).

> O the depth of the riches and wisdom and knowledge of God! How unsearchable are his judgements and how inscrutable his ways! (Rom 11:33)

> And the one who was seated on the throne said . . . "*It is done!* I am the Alpha and the Omega, the Beginning and the End" (Rev 21:5–6, NRSV adapt.).

> The peoples "shall sing of the ways of the Lord" (Ps 138:5a).

The history of religion asserts—it sounds irreverent and yet it is true—that YHWH is a *nomadic God*, a Leader of nomads. If we hold fast to this aspect of God's Name, God's Revelation on earth, if we remember well that the adjectives justice and mercy, wisdom and long-suffering belong to this Name, and if we keep in mind that this particular form and profile do not contradict Omnipotence, Omnipresence, and Omniscience—then this description "nomadic God" can testify to the way we acquire knowledge. From knowing God's Way we come to know God's essential divinity—and not the other way around. There are varieties in the presence of God: God is present in a different way with someone who is dying than with someone young who is celebrating the spring season of life. God is present in a different way in history compared to nature, different in the world compared to the church, different in the Word compared to the sign, but also

> *different today compared to former times.*

That is why the Ark accompanied Israel's army. It is why the "carrying poles" cannot be removed from God's mobile cherubim throne (Exod 25:15). It is why tension, friction, and, in the end, a mortal struggle took place in Canaan when the people came to a halt; between the God who Leads and Baal, the God of the Field. Those who are not nomadic in some form or fashion, literally or spiritually, do not know the way; they doze off under the sultry temptation of existing reality, the regular, cyclical rhythm of nature and rebirth.

God, YHWH, has a way. God makes room for the divine self and fashions people into fellow travelers to the eternal city. God commissions them as wanderers: not adventurers, not homebound, but faithful to the goal, obedient to the Word, watchful for the acts of the Lord. For this Restless One, who moves restlessly in spite of a peaceful essence, knows what that One wants in the midst of tumult.

5.

The *harrowing reality of history* depends on the unity of the Word of God and the Act of God, of saving word and saving event. Nature is not as real as this, not even in its darkest regions; nature knows no heaven or hell. Heaven and hell are endpoints not of natural existence but of historical life. History, in all its *magnificence*, becomes manifest in the Kingdom of God, and that kingdom itself grows within the fields of history, pouring out within history and spreading through it. An "eternal recurrence" could never bring forth something new; no chain of reincarnations can substitute for the gravity of purposeful history. Human beings move into history with inextinguishable *memory*; nations have, "make," and suffer history. The seal of concrete history is *politics*, the long-term struggle for justice within a community. The only reason this long road does not dissolve into madness is because God has a Way over the earth; because the Name employs Cyrus and Emperor Augustus and Pontius Pilate. If the Anti-Messiah, the Antichrist, is a political figure, a world-dominating person, the Messiah, the Christ, is no less political. Indeed, the counter-candidate would not aggrandize himself so much if the Messiah were not striding very decisively toward the world's throne along the way of God. Here, too, the word precedes: it is proclaimed to us, it is taught to us, and from out of that, history acquires its depth for faith—its harrowing and magnificent reality.

5a.

Listen to this worship song of Habakkuk "according to Shigionoth," which means, "the manner of those who rage" (Hab 3:1):

> God came from Teman,
> The Holy One from Mount Paran. Selah (= Worship!).
> His glory covered the heavens,
> And the earth was full of his praise . . .
> Before him went pestilence,
> And fever *in his footsteps.*
> He stood and measured the earth;
> He looked and startled the nations.
> And the everlasting mountains were scattered,
> The perpetual hills bowed low.

> The ways of ages are his ways . . .
> You split the earth with rivers.
> The mountains saw you, and writhed;
>   a torrent of water swept by;
> the deep gave forth its voice.
>   The sun raised high its hands;
> the moon stood still in its exalted place,
>   at the light of your arrows speeding by,
>   at the gleam of your flashing spear.
> *In fury you trod the earth,*
>   *in anger you threshed nations.*
> You came forth to save your people,
>   to save your anointed.
> You pierced with their own arrows the head of his warriors,
>   who came like a whirlwind to scatter us,
>   gloating as if ready to devour the poor who were in hiding.
> You trampled the sea with your horses,
>   churning the mighty waters.
> I hear, and I tremble within;
>   my lips quiver at the sound (Hab 3:3, 5–6, 9b–13a, 14–16a, NRSV adapt.).

Or, let us hear a profound conversation, in Exod 33:11–15; it contains "teaching" about the Way:

> The Lord used to speak to Moses face to face, as one speaks to a friend . . . Moses said to the Lord, "See, you have said to me, 'Bring up this people'; but you have not let me know whom you will send with me. Yet you have said, 'I know you by name, and you have also found favour in my sight.' Now if I have found favour in your sight, show me *your way*, so that I may know you and find favour in your sight. Consider too that this nation is your people." The Lord said, "Would my Face have to *go along*, to give you rest?" And Moses said to him, "If your Face will not go with us, do not carry us up from here" (NRSV, adapt.).

6.

Defenselessness and *powerlessness* bear the noblest appearance in this world. And God's Way "knows" yet more deeply the righteous, the poor, the orphan, the widow, justice, the "short work" (Rom 9:28b, KJV), the hope of the wretched, the turtledove (Ps 74:19), the apple of the eye (Ps

17:8; Zech 2:8). Word and Act serve to reach the End. They also serve to protect and preserve and deliver these powerless people and defenseless powers. The naked fact, so to speak, of God's existence, permanence, and endurance—as this very God, whose virtues we know through the Name, by the holy Teaching—not only illuminates history but also transforms it. God's work is not just speech, not just an act, but a *woorddaad*, word-act, and a *daadwoord*, act-word, which pursues a *course* across the earth, realizing its task, completing its project, an endeavor proportional in weight, and indeed more than proportional, to creation in the beginning. It is the creation of the End, of the Sabbath, through "the footsteps of the Anointed One" (Ps 89:51). These divine footsteps indicate and seal their own *history* within common history.

6a.

Once more—for it is clearer here than anywhere else in the holy Teaching—we understand this Way rightly only from the Middle; from the place where YHWH founded a memorial for the divine name (Exod 20:24); where God's trace in history has left an impression, and God's particular way has carved out a channel in the life of the people. These are nodal points that no one can fully forget: not because a holy past hovers around them, but because they continue to open up the Way and to disclose a future for the people. They are midpoints and media. They speak in the midst of time and proclaim that God is "holy," which is to say, different from the world and the gods. Finally, we are invited to hold fast to the memorial of that decisive Middle (2 Tim 2:8); to celebrate the life of Jesus as the holiest past and the holiest future. "Do this in remembrance of me" (Luke 22:19; 1 Cor 11:24), and "then you proclaim the Lord's death with an eye on his future" (1 Cor 11:26, NRSV adapt.; cf. Rev 3:20). In him the whole fullness of deity dwells bodily (Col 2:8), in him the Lord goes the way of all flesh (Josh 23:14; 1 Kgs 2:2), and yet it is, par excellence, *his* way. The Name in its humiliation, its descent into "the lower parts of the earth" (Eph 4:9) and its appearance "in the likeness of sinful flesh" (Rom 8:3), is itself called the Way. Such a Way stands parallel with Truth and Life: "I am the Way, and the Truth, and the Life" (John 14:6). Footsteps like these are pressed indelibly into the earth. They mark where God, this God, has taken up our life and our death, where God has joined us in our lot even into outer darkness. If we look back from Jesus Christ to the Old Testament, it *enlivens* the latter's testimony to the God who, afterward just as before, makes a way across the earth. This God will at the End complete the work and will be glorious in all the saints and in the world.

84   *Chapter 9*

7.

But, now notice this: the holy Teaching speaks about "God's way" in a different manner, namely as *synonymous with the fulfillment of God's commandments*.

"Make me to know your ways, O Lord" (Ps 25:4), that is, the ways in which I must go in order to please you. It is then not primarily my ways, although they are my deeds. And when they are called "God's ways," they are not disconnected from God's Way in the sense discussed above: from the course that strives in and against and to the end of history, they signify a *participation* in the Middle of fulfillment.

He leads the humble in what is right (Ps 25:9).

Teach me your way, O Lord,
   that I may walk in your truth;
   give me an undivided heart to revere your name (Ps 86:11).

I delight in the way of your decrees
   as much as in all riches (Ps 119:14).

They have not known my ways (Heb 3:10 quoting Ps 95:10).

And in the Acts of the Apostles, "the way of the Lord" comes to mean the teaching, that is, the proclamation concerning Christ, the life of the church of Christ, in short: we would say *Christianity* (if we can still use this word without causing any misunderstanding) as human history.

Acts 18:25 and following: about Apollos, he was taught in the way of the Lord (i.e., "knowing only of the baptism of John")—and when Aquila and Priscilla heard him, they took him aside and explained to him the *way of God* more deeply and more adequately. And Saul persecutes those who are "of this way" (i.e., of that faith, of that sect [Acts 9:2])—and at Ephesus those who attend the synagogue begin to speak evil "of the way" (Acts 19:9), and later there is no small commotion "because of the way" (19:23).

The Way, that is, sacred history as *God's* history; "our way" answers to God's history and is linked to it by a mysterious connection . . . "Our way" is the course of confession and the action of the community in the world.

It cannot possibly be the same word by accident; God's Way and our way correspond; God's Way is in the end described with the verbs from the Apostle's Creed: received, born, suffered, crucified, died, buried, *descended—resurrected*, ascended, seated, coming. Correspondingly, "our way" will describe the same course: from the "station of humiliation" to the "station of exaltation."

We are therefore always of good courage (2 Cor 5:6, 8; RSV).

Sacred history encompasses world history! Because sacred history breaks through the "eternal recurrence," the roadless acts, the cycle of things and reveals YWHW as the Godhead.

Chapter 10

Sanctification

1.

If a young girl at boarding school becomes infatuated with a book—isn't it because she sees herself reflected in one of the main characters, whose dreams are the same as her dreams? And the boy scout, what does he find in Karl May? The vast reality of adventure and service, where he is an as-yet-unknown hero. The elderly gentleman looks to the book for a holy past, which he opens with awe and devotion on quiet evenings. The mature spirit understands that their chosen book conveys the essence of human life that they, unbeknownst to themselves, have lived through. It is a rich and sad universe of eternal movement within a living endurance, this one thing: to be human—"O, the fraught, labored gasp arising from a moment hid in my chest"[1]—to be oneself, to be with everything.

But now, about the Bible. We carry no weight in the Bible. We are being pushed out of place. We are being overlooked. Our personal portrait is not in it, neither the reflection of our dream, nor the image of our life's adventure, nor the justification of our secret past. The earth is there like a ballast, and humans, seen from behind, appear to be fugitives, disobedient animals; the lofty spirit leans on crutches, and there is a cruel estrangement-from-ourselves in the summer day of our radiant energy—and from the side one hears of awful behavior, a chaos full of traitors' gestures and gnashing of teeth over lost life; and even pity, the silent, mild weeping for ourselves, in which we still abide in the shadow of death, has an end. We just can't believe that when the Book-of-Books is opened, the book of *our* life, which does us good to leaf through, *will close* (cf. Rev 20:12).

Enough about God! Let us hear something about humankind! Come closer to "real life," stay closer to home! Thus some readers who have made it this far will resentfully speak. But resist this entrapment, you who wish to be educated by the holy Teaching. We find in the biblical ABCs, in the *grondbestek* or ground-design, that humans are *constantly*, indirectly spoken of, exactly when God, *this* God, is named. Conversely, too, when humans are spoken of, God is at hand. When the story tells of Abel or Melchizedek, or Cain or Sennacherib, or the pregnancy of Rachel, or the siege of Jerusalem, it is, in the last analysis, a story about God and nothing but God. No proportionality applies here: the order cannot be reversed, and on just this account, we have to do with the *holy* Teaching. "Holy" in the Bible cuts off proportionality. This is why the Bible is such a strange and vexing book; it does not glorify humanity, and it hardly even appreciates humans as partner to God; lots of action takes place over their heads. Humans are present but incidental to the main drama. Such is the case not only in the case of wicked people, but also the pious; actually, pious people come even less into their own than do the wicked in their conceit. All people are *ordinary* people. The Bible does not believe that faithful people are not also ordinary people. As for so-called saints or "holy ones," yes, they are indeed a class of their own. But how exactly are they different? That is precisely the question we seek now to answer. Above all, they are *very* ordinary people according to our perception and judgment. We can already understand this a bit when we compare it to our common use of the phrase, "holy land." We do not consider a land "holy" because of the moral qualities of its soil; this would be nonsense. But even if we factor in the inhabitants of this land, we know that it can never have been anything too special, but rather, religiously speaking, somewhat backward, hardly uplifting, and even, one might say, banal.

The holy land is not a land of devout people. It is an ordinary land; however, we cannot reverse this statement and say that all ordinary countries can be or become "holy." The word "holy" is derived in the Bible's language from the

VERB "to sanctify," or make holy

and not vice versa! Let us keep that in mind. There is no quality of "holiness" whose distribution the above verb expresses. The verb is the root-word, and the adjective derives from it. Does this seem to you like splitting hairs? It is not so: we touch here on theological questions of the highest order. Although we cannot explore the matter in depth, I still believe the reader will in this presentation perceive something of the wonderful and liberating knowledge that lies in this question—and what a fine resource has been given to us to distinguish between biblical and pagan teaching.

What is holy has been made holy, or sanctified: and to sanctify means to *separate* something or someone, to set it apart, to make it available, to consecrate, to requisition it for use. The meaning of these usages comes immediately into focus: holy day, holy supper, and holy person. These have, in the first instance, nothing to do with a moral standard. Rather, the adjective indicates: here we encounter something profane, which is nevertheless separated by God from the rest of profane existence, *so that it may be a witness to God's own virtues*. What is called "holy" is indeed nothing special in itself—as, for example, the desert sand where Moses stood (Exod 3:5). It did not differ in any way from the rest of the immeasurable steppes, but something from God *happens*, and that is why the same narrative says: "remove the sandals from your feet, for the place on which you are standing is holy ground!" If we on our human side have no basis for declaring the profane as holy, this is due to the fact that the quality "holy" springs exclusively from the *action* of "making holy."

Strangely enough, the pagan religious sensibility also distinguishes between the profane and the sacred. We may set aside the question whether that which is sacred according to the pagans coincides with what the Bible calls holy—the decisive difference lies herein: that pagan religion holds the *sources* and *summits* of Life to be sacred in themselves. The pagan discovers or declares that blood, sexual power, fecundity, hearth and home, wine and tournaments, war and state are "holy," which is to say, imbued with an aura of power.

Finally, the pagan glorifies the *All*. By glorifying the sources and summits, the pagan in the end glorifies the primal forces as a totality. Whenever Existence is experienced in its shocking and overwhelming aspect, there the pagans "bow down"; it says in Exod 20:5, "You shall not bow down to them or worship them." Literally it reads, "you shall not *prostrate* yourself," that is, before the images of sacred power.

The Name of God signifies the disenchantment of the world: the denial that what exists, no matter how powerful, could be sacred in itself and, as such, deserving of divine worship. It is God who effects sanctification. That is—for the pagan sensibility—nothing else than

sabotage!

YHWH does indeed boast of being the Spoilsport, the first and the last. I read somewhere that a person who professes to be Christian first and Dutch second should be considered a saboteur.[2] Well, this confession is so self-evident that the church has never thought otherwise; this confession belongs to the church's very being. It is nonsense to dispute this obvious truth, but for the unchurched it is *not* obvious.

Precisely this is the pivotal subject matter of the Bible—and we should discern the meaning behind this nonsense. It is not the people who believe but rather *God* who is from the outset Saboteur, Underminer, Disperser, Lampoonist of nature when it inflates itself to godhood. God is the great Mutineer (Isa 8:13), *because* God desires to be the Savior and Redeemer of the poor, afflicted creature.

2.

To start as close to home as possible, let's look back to the beginning, the section about the "Teaching." The language of the Bible demands respect here; it deals with the veracity of the action, the accuracy of the *verb*. The expression "holy," predicated on the Teaching or instruction, applies in the same sense. The instruction serves our sanctification, and for that reason it has become exceptional and so receives the designation "holy." The Name itself sanctifies us, and the Name wishes to be sanctified on the earth. People whom God has requisitioned are therefore called holy. If it can be said of all the biblical terms in the old dogmatics denoting the different stages of God's saving work—calling, regeneration, conversion, justification, sanctification—that they can be traced back to the streambed of biblical language as *pars pro toto*, each part representing the whole, the word "sanctification" has such an *expansive place* in Scripture that this *pars pro toto* relationship applies particularly to it. This is how

HUMANS COME INTO VIEW

as objects of a specific divine endeavor. Sanctification expresses not just a part, and a decisive part, of God's saving work, but rather this part indicates the whole. The impatient reader can be reassured: we humans come hereby to our turn. Even more than that: we are the whole point. Human nature, as it is, and although it is as it is, must come into contact with God and all the divine virtues, and through such contact, it bears witness to the divine virtues. Already human nature emerges when Adam and Eve appear from the shrubbery and stand in the Light of Love, which is judgment. It begins with the call: *Adam, where are you?*

Calvin tends to put all the emphasis on this meaning of sanctification, which includes many forms of "obedience." But the Bible goes much further in this direction, drawing from deeper and holding it longer.

3.

Here we come across so weighty a letter of the spiritual alphabet that anyone who understands it understands almost everything; they have become ready for independent reading and learning. On the other hand, those who do not have a *simple eye* will soon have, not the opposite, namely, a complicated eye, but rather an *evil eye* (Matt 6:23, KJV). It has long since become clear that we will not be able to complete the biblical ABCs within the parameters of this book. But virtually everything that remains outstanding is contained within the right understanding of *this* matter, or better, this act: of sanctification. And once we grasp this truth, we can hardly resist the feeling of a certain completeness! The simplicity that we discussed in the chapter on "Teaching" becomes very clear and convincing at this point.

Let us now glance around and make note of other *oer-woorden* or primary words, which we have so far only glossed over or discussed in passing. What, for example, do these words mean?

Covenant, Flesh, Spirit, World?

What is the meaning of the shape and form of

priest, prophet, king, temple, sacrifice?

These words cannot be approached unless one begins from "sanctification," considered not as a ledger line or explanation but rather as a definite and decisive action of God, of this God. We will see "sanctification" appear again and again, and each time distinctly, yet it is, in essence, single and recognizable.

4.

You will naturally ask: how is it sensible for *God's self* to be called holy, if the foregoing is true and adequate to the subject matter? How can it be said of God that God is exceptional, or separated, or set apart? And yet we cannot for an instant lose contact with that fundamental meaning and so become lost. If we do, we slip into cold abstraction: "God is God." Or we plunge into disrespect: "dear Lord," which is to say, "obliging, tractable Lord." Yes, the Lord is called holy: because this One is distinguished as the Other *in* the world, *from* the world. Or, more clearly: *this* God is God. It is YHWH, the Father of our Lord Jesus Christ, who claims and wills to be God, only and ever as such, through all eternity and in every second of time. Exactly this comprises the virtue that we name as "holiness."

When we broke away from equating "sacred" with moral, pure, or upstanding, many fell back on the idea that the holiness of God consists in "infinite distance"; in the horror and abyss of the Absolute. The Bible, however, constantly connects holiness with revelation, nearness, action, industriousness, election, covenant; with joining and being led by the Lord. The "Holy One" is the God to whom there is no road—but this is just the negative side of the positive, saving message: through God's acts, God distinguishes God's self *in* the world, *from* the world, and God thereby travels the road to humankind.

Holy, holy, holy is
the Lord of Hosts;

which means, the Ruler of Powers, the Leader of History,

and, as if that were not clear enough to indicate God's proximity, the angelic song continues (Isa 6:3):

the whole earth is full of his glory.

Rightly understood, this means that the world, which in itself is not divine, is saturated with the radiance of divine nearness; this is the vision of the seraphim, the angels, who are singing there. But they also see, and, in the same breath they proclaim, the foundation of that grace: that God wills through *actions* to distinguish God's self from everything that happens in the world. We can clarify the significance of this statement no better than by citing the word that is written in Hosea (11: 9):

I will not execute my fierce anger . . .
for I am God and no mortal,
the Holy One in your midst.

The "Holiness" in this oracle (about "the Holy One") betokens *wonder*: wonder that God does not loose the divine displeasure; wonder that celebrates God's decision to remain near, "in your midst." God's holiness results, then, in chastisement that is "awesome in splendor" (Exod 15:11; Ps 111:9) as well as salvation (Pss 22:4, 5; 89:19; 105:3) and answering prayer (Pss 3:5; 20:7; 28:2). This is the reason why—it cannot be repeated enough—God's holiness belongs to God's presence. Nearness is the wellspring of astonishment, and yet also the reason why such astonishment is not arbitrary or magical or sensational; it is the everlasting earnest or pledge offered up to every moment. Astonishment can reflect either horror or joy, and neither gives less witness to the holiness of God than the other.

The guilty fugitive Jacob is astonished at his vision of the ladder of light, upon which angels ascend and descend, and he expects judgment.

Conversely, twenty years later, he experiences a demon-like attack from God in the middle of the night, just when he had attained, so to speak, a better life (Gen 28:12; 32:24). Both moments were revelations of God's holiness; the radiance of holiness shines in one and storms in the other.

5.

Behold! As *this* God, who alone is "Godhead," God sanctifies a day; a loaf of bread; a land, a way, a people, a human, a house, a book. God requisitions these to glorify the divine virtues, God's own qualities in opposition to all gods, powers, and principalities that also exist or appear to exist (Exod 20:11; 19:6; 1 Sam 21:6; Num 16:3; Lev 27:21; Matt 24:15; 1 Cor 6:2; 7:14; Eph 1:18; Col 1:12; 1 Peter 1:16, 2:9, etc.). God wills for each of the above-listed items to be as they were meant to be from the beginning. God wills to purge them from sin, the flesh, the world, the "spiritual forces of evil in the heavenly places" (Eph 6:12), the "cares of the world" (Matt 13:22), the "the desire of the eyes" (1 John 2:16). God *wills to release them* from the thrall of the gods and the pagan powers.

We have moved on, almost unawares, from discussing holy things to holy people; and that is helpful, since it is for the sake of humankind that God sanctifies the list of objects above, though it is also true—without contradiction—that God has done this work of setting apart to exalt God's own Name and Revelation. What, then, does the sanctification of *humankind* entail? May we put it this way . . . ? After all, we are not writing a dogmatic study or a systematic theology, but we are spelling out the biblical ABCs. *God makes the elect people*

into UNBELIEVING PEOPLE,

namely, in their relation to the world and all its gods. God seizes them and awakens them from the indolence of the flesh; God takes them and gives them a view of God's virtues and actions. God sets them apart and shows them the road that God travels, the way of the Anointed One. God addresses them and gives them the *word* and puts praise in their hearts. God lays a hand on their body and teaches them, so that their members no longer serve "impurity and greater and greater iniquity" but rather "righteousness for sanctification" (Rom 6:19).

That calling may be a long road, like a trek through the desert, or like running a racecourse, except that what *happens* reaches further and proceeds faster. The Bible says: something from God happens to a person, around a person, and it is wonderful: an ordinary human receives an extraordinary—*assignment*, which upholds itself, how exactly, nobody knows, least of all that human. The person is God's servant, God's "fellow worker," God's child and the apple of God's eye, although in and of themselves, such a one is nothing too special. The Bible shows no great interest in substances, properties, characteristics, principles. Instead it attends to what has happened; is *happening*. It matters that something *happens*.

God approaches us in God's acts, and we, too, act. From where do these human acts arise? Whether a change of essence has taken place, or whether these people are really "changed"—and in what sense—we will come back to later when we have time to "theologize." Scripture itself asks—notice—directly: "What has happened? What is taking place?" "I will be with you as I shall be with you" (Exod 3:14). How? Well, you will find out: God's being can be found nowhere else than in what God *does*. Likewise also the sanctified human: this person can be found nowhere else than in what they do.

The beginning and the principle of it all is *the divine gift of unbelief*, just as God's own existence is itself the constant, creative denial of the divine power of nature, of fallen angels, of pharaohs and heroes. *This* God signifies the disenchantment of the world; and the sanctification that this God effects is the de-divinization, the disenchantment of the world on our behalf. May this unbelief continue to grow, so that it becomes our "second nature." Yes indeed, it makes for a long road, a struggle, a process, and that is exactly what the word sanctification, in its narrower sense, entails.

6.

Now, many will think: this still seems very *negative* to me! *But is it really*? Have we forgotten what we have heard about the Name and about the order of the divine virtues? Isn't the Name the Revelation of the abundance of the Lord? And isn't the abundance of the Name present within each virtue, each perfection?

The holiness of God cannot possibly be a limitation or an addition to God's grace or mercy. We remember what we heard about the unity of the virtues, which is Love. Although "love" is just a human word, and so makes confusion possible, the divine love should *not* be mistaken for any other powers of love in the world. To protect against that eventuality, *therefore* it is proclaimed and taught to us: "God is holy, God sanctifies; be holy, for I am holy!" The sovereignty of God issues in God's "meddling" with us—and yet it would not appear to us as *God's* sovereignty if God were not faithful to God's own self; if God's turning to us did not differ from that of Zeus or Odin, Brahma or Fate. But it does differ, because God's loving is noncompulsory, unforced, nonnecessary, free. It consists in a constant, creative denial of divine power, for the sake of those whom God has called.

So if God makes us *unbelieving*, God does it on the basis of the divine compassions. If God sanctifies us in the world, God does it because God has "loved us with an everlasting love" (Jer 31:3). If God appoints us to a new service, it is because God has become our *Redeemer*. The "Holy One of Israel" is the selfsame who is also called *Goel*, Redeemer (Isa 41:14; 43:3; 47:4; 48:17; 49:7; 54:5). God's people hallow the divine Name since they see what God's hands have accomplished in the midst of them (Isa 29:23). In many places in the Bible one can, in place of "holiness"—and without changing the basic meaning—read *grace*. We see therein an important piece on the letter board of the biblical ABCs.

The Holiness of God is God's own self-setting-apart. Though near at hand and good and doing good, God is God and *goes along God's own way*. Also and precisely insofar as God, in the power of the Name and the names by which we call on God, self-reveals as Immanuel (with us is God), God remains the Lord; the Other; self-sufficing and glorious in God's self. And that is also beneficial for our salvation, since it guarantees that grace has a divine foundation, and God's nearness has a divine depth, and our unbelief toward the gods has a divine reason.

7.

We may best approach the idea of the *covenant* from this vantage. It was founded! It came from *one side*; and yet it establishes, preserves, and protects a *reciprocity* between God and humans. What reciprocity? This one, which exists according to the rule:

BE HOLY, BECAUSE I AM HOLY;

be different, for I am different. Deny what I deny, choose what I choose, and reject what I reject. See, I have brought you out of the house of bondage to demons.

REMAIN WITH YOUR DELIVERER.

Therefore, you shall have no other gods; do not make an idol. Leave behind the pagan prostration, the bowing low, the throwing of oneself down before the divine powers. Do not use my Name, my Revelation, for your profane purposes and trivial concerns. "Sanctify" the day that proclaims that I, not you, bring the world to completion. And you shall respect your parents, because I have appointed them, and have regard for your neighbor's life and marriage and holdings and good name. These are the *Ten Commandments*, through which one "keeps the covenant." They are the methods of persevering in covenant.

If you remain with me, you will have no need to grovel again before the powers or to violate the body and soul and life of your fellow human. You will have life and abundance.

"Calling" and "election" can be agonizing enough, as is the case, for example, with a genius in the midst of a hostile environment. But the glory outweighs these sufferings by far and beyond all measure (cf. 2 Cor 4:17). So it must be with Israel—though the parallel is only partial. It is by no means a sinecure to be God's chosen one, but the glory surpasses the hardship that it brings with it. Because this is so, and to reveal it as such, the commandments are given, an additional gift of grace. God also sanctifies through the forgiveness of sins. Perhaps nowhere else does God distinguish the divine self more strongly *in* the world *from* the world than in the forgiveness of sins. For this is binding: "There is forgiveness with you, *so that* you may be feared" (Ps 130:4).

Now then, be holy, because I am holy! From now on, remain with your Redeemer!

BE DIFFERENT,

by being "holy," or, what amounts to the same, by remaining with me, who has graciously called and chosen and covered you with forgiveness. This "remaining" is "keeping the covenant," "keeping the commandments," "sanctifying the Name."

7a.

The moment has come when we may boldly present a series of biblical texts one after the other, which, if we had begun with them, might have shocked and confused. We note the following word usages:

Lev 21:7: They are holy to *their God*.
Lev 27: it shall be holy to the Lord as a devoted field (v. 21); All tithes from the land . . . are the Lord's; they are holy to the Lord (v. 30; cf. also v. 32).
Num 5:17: the priest shall take holy water (cf. Lev 16:4; 1 Sam 21:6; Exod 29:34, 37).
Num 16:3: All the congregation are holy, *every one* of them.
Num 16:5: In the morning the Lord will make known who is *his*, and who is holy.
Num 16:7: whom the Lord *chooses* shall be the holy one.

Furthermore, something quite different, yet based on the same *grondvorm*, ground-form:

"They set apart [that is: sanctified] Kedesh in Galilee" (Josh 20:7), so that it would be a city of refuge for a person who commits manslaughter, killing though without "hand upraised" (Num 15:30), that is, without malice aforethought.
"The Levites had to slaughter the Passover lamb for everyone who was not clean, to make it holy to the Lord" (2 Chr 30:17).
"Set them apart for war against her!" (Jer 6:4, Christian Standard Bible)
"I will set apart destroyers against you" (Jer 22:7, Christian Standard Bible)
"Her profit and her prostitute's wages will be holiness to the Lord" (Isa 23:18, NASB adapt.); the profits from Tyre will have another destination, namely, they will be dedicated to God's people.

In a more spiritual application, but still using the same *grondvorm*, ground-form:

Exod 19:6: *you shall be for me a holy nation.*
Ps 89:5: your faithfulness in the assembly of the holy ones.
1 Cor 7:14: For the unbelieving husband is made holy through his wife.
Dan 7:18: But the holy ones of the Most High shall receive the kingdom.
Lev 22:32: You shall not profane my holy name, that I may be sanctified among the people of Israel: I am the Lord; I sanctify you.
Ezek 20:12; cf. 37:28: Moreover I gave them *my* sabbaths, as a sign between me and them, so that they might know that I the Lord sanctify them.
1 Cor 1:2: To the church of God that is in Corinth, to those who are sanctified in Christ Jesus, called to be saints.
1 Cor 3:17: For God's temple is holy, and you are that temple.
2 Cor 13:12: All the holy ones greet you.

Now, finally, we are approaching the middle:

Jesus prays: "*Sanctify them in the truth*; your word is truth" (John 17:17).
"And for their sakes I sanctify myself, so that they also may be sanctified in truth" (v. 19)!!

That is, the *sacrifice* that differs from all other sacrifices in that (a) the one who sacrifices and the sacrifice are identical; and (b) the sacrifice is made not only symbolically, but literally, truly, vicariously.
And in Heb 2:10–11 we read:

> It was fitting that God, for whom and through whom all things exist, in bringing many children to glory, should make the pioneer of their salvation perfect through sufferings. For the one who sanctifies and those who are sanctified *are all of one*. For this reason Jesus is not ashamed to call them brothers and sisters.

And even the demons call out to Christ: "I know who you are, the Holy One of God" (Mark 1:24).

And the apostles write to us: "you holy ones!—all the holy ones greet you!"

8.

In response to the sanctification that is an act of God, humans know that they are called to sanctify the day, the congregation, the tithes, the offerings, the war, the body—and to sanctify themselves, which is to say, to set themselves apart for service to God, *this* God, whose Name they know and whose virtues they praise. The self-sanctifying of humans because of God's prior sanctifying of them means, first of all, joy: joy over emancipation from the yoke of the world, from the laws of "strange religions" (in the sense of the Belgic Confession §34; cf. Lev 20:7; Jer 6:4). This dimension of sanctification is most clearly revealed in the *theocracy*, the ordering of life and state according to which the people of God seek to make their common life a sign of God's will.

Humans sanctify *themselves* because they are sanctified. They are already consecrated, confronted, called, chosen. Therefore they repent, insofar as they believe that they have already received forgiveness. When a person sanctifies themselves, they sanctify their *life*, their *work*, their marriage, their friendship, the society for which they are responsible.

After all, the human is not an ethereal figure, nor a purely spiritual being. They do not merely exist and then, secondarily, add activity to this existence as if it were a role to play. No, in the Bible, the human *is* their life, their act *is* their *being* ("act" here signifying quite comprehensively). On this account, no domain can be left untouched. God has *interfered* with humans and their world; and, with another and just as necessary emphasis: *God* has interfered with this human and their world. If God is a *particular* God, God is also and as such, Elohim, the Deity! Likewise, sanctification is a particular sanctification, but also and as such, sanctification extends into—well, how better to put it?—life; the world—in totality. What this means in praxis is another question. But whether one makes a start, whether one suffers from failure—that is decisive!

8a.

It is possible to say what sanctification consists in—that sanctification by which humans sanctify themselves. But everything that is said about it will immediately skew if we understand the moral life, the cleansing of the soul, the purification of our actions, our growth in love and patience and all virtues, *otherwise* than how they must be understood. The biblical ABCs teach us that "holy" has nothing in itself to do with moral qualities. How then does holiness work?

Humankind is not a thing, not a time interval, not a cultic object. Humankind is a moral being. In view of that, sanctification, which is to say, separation, acquires the specific content that is laid out in the *commandments* and *admonitions* of Scripture. Because humans are moral, responsible, self-directing creatures, sanctification has a dual and dramatic character. Because in the Bible's view humans live in a covenant relationship with YHWH, the act of separation comes originally from one side; it is a divine action. And yet this does not preclude that, within this previously constituted covenant, humans enjoy a reciprocal relationship. Humans effect the actions that the Spirit and the human spirit indicate—though even here, the fact that humans desire to sanctify themselves does not cease to be a gracious calling from God.

9.

FAITH

The human whom the Bible takes seriously is the one who is sanctified. Besides this set-apart human, other persons come into view only as a transparency for the mirror of revelation.

A human is called "holy" when, by virtue of a divine initiative, they are no longer left to themselves; they can no longer simply be themselves, they can no longer believe in their own self-actualization. Rather, surrounded by God's favor and judgment, estranged from the profane and also from their own natural religion, they begin to live by *faith*. Faith is the acceptance of sanctification. As such, intellectual assent, mystical trust, and moral willing, which together constitute faith, are one and the same action.

It is exactly in *this* connection that we must speak of "faith." Like almost all biblical *oerwoorden*, primary words, "faith" grows up along the wall of sanctification and in the furrows that it has drawn. But the word "faith" is also uniquely and constantly misunderstood and misused; it has become a kind of shrill automated tick. We would do well to practice our attentiveness and to sharpen our senses so that we set the adjective "holy" before every biblical *grondwoord*, ground-word. It always fits, since sanctification is so central in the Bible—yet it is nowhere more useful than before the word "faith."

Faith is *holy* faith: a particular acceptance, assent, trust, and expectation. It is an answer to the call. It is acknowledging the Name, which is holy. It is praise of the divine virtues, which are particular; a following of the divine acts, which are holy; a listening to the holy Word, a trust in the holy Way. That is how faith itself can be called "holy." This world teems with faith and religiosity, in which we can count on so little, and yet we must go on. People "believe" in God, in the Good, in our better selves, in evolution, in the value of our nation, in the power of the state, in humanity, in the future. They must put faith in these things, if they are able. The Bible in the meantime talks about *the* faith, *holy* faith. And so—just so!—faith, hope, and love *abide*!

In the eyes of the Messiah, the Christ, faith is the only good thing in this sinful world. He, Christ, is *the* Act of God. In him the virtues of God have manifested to us for our benefit. He is the Name. He is himself the Word. His way leads to the rightful end of history, which begins with "that holy thing" (Luke 1:35, KJV).

9a.

FLESH and SPIRIT

"Faith," like "Covenant," belongs to the same linguistic domain as "holy" and "sanctification." We see that more clearly if we heed the contrast of *"flesh"* and *"spirit"* in the Bible.

"Flesh" is

    a all living beings (Gen 9:17, "all flesh");
    b human beings in their aspect as creatures (Num 16:22);
    c human beings in their alienation from God (John 3:6; Rom 7:18).

"Spirit" on the other hand means that which belongs to God.

> Cursed are those who (. . .) make mere flesh their strength (Jer 17:5).
> The Egyptians are human, and not God;
>   their horses are flesh, and not spirit (Isa 31:3).
> What is born of the flesh is flesh—If you sow to your own flesh, you will reap
>   corruption from the flesh (John 3:6; Gal 6:8).

The flesh remains immersed in the existing, in the visible, in the primordial, in itself, in lust; or also in virtue, in the letter, in the form. "Flesh" is the unknowing resistance of the soul. The works of the flesh include "heresies" (Gal 5:20, KJV), something we consider to be eminently spiritual.

But take note of this: "flesh" is never the carnal drive as such. And "spirit" never means "the inner person." The spirit is God, as God sanctifies the flesh. There you have it! And so closes the circle of truth, the compass of our efforts to understand the special place of the word "holy" in the biblical ABCs. The Spirit is not a fragment or direction or characteristic of our nature and does not *become* that, either. This follows directly from everything we have heard about holy land, holy day, holy war, holy tithes, and so on. But the Spirit of God bears witness with our spirit that we are children of God—as it was said to Moses: "see, the place where you are standing is holy ground" (Exod 3:5), because something *happens* there, someone is requisitioned. In that place, I am at work, the Holy Spirit, and no human ghost, no Israelite or Christian spirit, but the wholly other Spirit who performs its own work of separating-out upon you. You know of it, and you believe in it, and you are not deceived: the Spirit testifies again with your spirit that you are children of God (Rom 8:16).

We read in Rom. 8:29a, 30–31:

> For those whom he foreknew he also predestined to be conformed to the image of his Son . . . And those whom he predestined he also called; and those whom he called he also justified; and those whom he justified he also glorified. What then are we to say about these things? If God is for us, who is against us?

That is sanctification! All of this together, a single, unique divine *action* of separation and setting apart, altogether constituting one salvation. God is *for* us, not against us, as we might otherwise have expected.

For God is OTHER.

10a.

It is striking, but it cannot come as a surprise to the somewhat initiated, that "flesh" in its third meaning (humans in their alienation from God) becomes far-reaching and critical only in the New Testament. Excepting one or two allusions, the person of Adam does not appear in the Old Testament after Gen 2–4, and the Old Testament nowhere associates human nature with the Fall—but in light of the *second Adam*, Jesus Christ (1 Cor 15:47), the first Adam takes on fresh importance and visibility. In a similar way, only the gift of the *Spirit* qualifies humankind as "flesh," and, in that aspect, merits condemnation and rejection. God's self-revelation reveals the human, too: perforce, God's showing of the divine self also shows what humankind really is. The apostle sees that reality and, by Christ's commission, communicates it: this is what the human really is. Only now does this become manifest.

Although the term "flesh" sounds weighty, it contains a hardly utterable and, empirically speaking, empty judgment; like the word "unholy," it is, as a concept, defined entirely by negation: it means, unconsecrated; not separated out; not set apart from the chaotic intermingling of the world. This judgment also therefore denies that sin is a substance, a thing, or an energy. We are instructed thereby, that sin is in no way a reality like creation is. *The Spirit reveals what flesh is*; we could not know it in advance.

"You are mine," God said to God's children, as God had said about the temple mount, "I desired it for my habitation" (cf. Pss 68:16; 132:13), and as God had said about the elect people, "this is the apple of my eye and my inheritance" (cf. Deut 32:10).

There lives a *qahal*, Hebrew for congregation, on earth, an *edah*, a church; they have a law, but it is a holy, wholly other law from the law of the nations. They have a country, but it is a holy, wholly other country, because something happens there that happens nowhere else. They have a sacrifice, but it is a holy, wholly other sacrifice, because this offering to God is a gift of God ("we give it to you as from your hand"; 1 Chr 29:14b), and it reconciles God to the one who presents it as their atoning sacrifice. And, by the same miracle, they are people, but holy, wholly other people, since they are taken up into *a wholly-other relationship with God*, namely, the covenant.

10b.

What does it all, cumulatively, mean? We can only indicate the relationships—without filling in their content. We can say only that to which the grammar points. To claim that a people, or a person, or a life is "holy," is no different than to say: this people, this person, this life

no longer finds its meaning in itself,

and even less so in the gods. Rather, it finds meaning only in God, *this* God, who is the God of the future. Therefore: keeping the covenant means that one does not fall back into a "self-standing" existence. The prophets did not demand that Israel should be a genuine, noble, pure, independent, or powerful people—only that they would be *God's* people. The same applies to all lives, and to all forms of life that are called "holy." *Each according to its own kind* must belong to God.

This piece of the biblical ABCs is difficult to understand; but woe to those who err in this regard, by seeking to make sense of it by a logic other than that of the Name. *This* God is our God, and this One is the Actor who has made us actors also. Something *happens*, on both sides. One side precedes and predominates, but nonetheless, the event occurs truly for both. Such is not the case with "holy land" or "holy showbread" (Exod 25:30); it holds true only for the holy human. These humans will no longer belong to themselves. There is a paradox here that can confuse us, but it cannot be simplified without introducing further confusion into the ABCs. The paradox consists in this: while preserving human nature, this sanctified human has nothing left but relationship, covenantal relationship, to God. Only with this consideration firmly in mind can we accept that moral cleansing coincides with sanctification, since humans are moral-spiritual beings that enjoy freedom in virtue of their creation. The paradox hence applies to humankind in particular: freedom being in human nature, the human chooses no longer for themselves. Whoever "loses their life" (Matt 10:39) gains freedom; and with this freedom, the human decides for dependence and no longer has life in themselves. It will not matter that such as one is a man, but that he is "a man of God," as the Pastoral Letters say (1 Tim 6:11).

In discussing these matters—"spiritual things" as we call them—we must never even for a moment forget that the Bible cannot be read as "pagan" or "Jewish." Neither is it an explanation of the world, nor a kind of sacred jurisprudence. It is proclamation: proclamation of the covenant. Scripture tells and tells and tells again *how it happened*: when Abraham, when Jacob, when David, when Peter, when Lydia the saleswoman of purple fabrics, when Timothy joined in the work of *this* God with heart and body, soul and sinew: in a word, how God sanctified them. That happened; it stands written. The accounts of this event are read, recited, chanted. They are heard, accepted, believed as the Name, as *the* Revelation. Those who are called in the same way as these forebears praise this event as their deliverance and the foundation of "the realm of freedom"; for they are called to "proclaim the virtues of him who called them out of darkness into his marvelous light" (1 Pet 2:9).

11.

That is why *remembering*, "not-forgetting," "setting it before one's eyes" is the order of the day. The Bible teems with admonitions not to forget: the benefits, the election, the exodus, the resurrection, the miracles, the commandments, and especially the covenant!

Sin—ah, who will permanently deliver this word from its ambience of societal indecency!—is not unvirtuous deeds or immoral acts, but rather

BREAKING THE COVENANT.

Sin is not remembering to Whom one belongs; not realizing what it means to be sanctified or set apart as a sign pointing to the divine virtues.

In contrast to Islam, which is the religion of achievement par excellence, the Bible views morality, keeping the commandments, as a *sign* of faithfulness: a proof of human "remembrance." That is why it is difficult to find a preference in the Old Testament for "higher," moral commandments over against cultic commandments, as, for example, the commandment to keep the Sabbath. Even in the writings of the prophets, who fulminate against self-enclosed, formal worship, we never encounter this distinction such that it would satisfy our modern hierarchy of values. In the prophets, too, the "lesser," the cultic, is itself the "greater," or a symbol of the "greater."

It all seems rather strangely mingled. In the Bible, there are no higher or lower ideals. There are duties—but not heavy and light duties; all are *equally heavy* or *equally light*, because they are all signs. "Heavy burdens" are imposed by those who no longer understand the entire Law; to the simple, this is said: "my yoke is easy, and my burden is light" (Matt 11:30), and from the community comes this echo: "His commandments are not heavy" (1 John 5:3, Douay-Rheims). Why not? Because the commandments are fulfilled whenever a person *remembers* what God has *accomplished*, and to Whom they belong.

12.

Perhaps no word is more suited to round out our impression of "sanctification" than the verb

TO SERVE.

To serve God has both (a) a "cultic" and (b) a "moral" sense. It means, first of all, to participate in temple worship, to make offering, and to give praise. It also, secondly, means to keep the commandments concerning the needs and rightful claims of one's neighbor. We now understand that this twofold sense of serve does not entail some primitive overestimation of the cult, but rather, it represents the abiding structure of the Ten Commandments, and the principal meaning of the first and second table.

If what we have heard about "holy" and "sanctification" is correct, then the service of God, or worship, can be nothing else than the source of all virtues.

Here, too, everything derives from the true God, about whose Name and Virtues and Actions we have heard. Those who "serve" the gods and worship them consider as "virtues" that which is contrary to the meaning of the covenant. Whoever stands in the wrong temple, also stands wrongly in life at large. Those who honor Nature and Power cannot but tread upon and violate their neighbor, eradicating the inferior, despising the weak, scorning the counsel of the righteous and overpowering logic.

The Law came together with the Sanctuary into this world. And they leave the world *together*, stranding us in the world-in-itself. First, the sanctuary is destroyed, then law and justice follow (Exod 3:12; 1 Sam 2:11; Ps 2:11; Mal 3:14, 18; Luke 2:37; Rom 7:6; 12:11; Phil 3:3; Col 3:24; Rom 14:18).

13.

In just this connection, the word "WORLD" is relevant. It has a parallel development with "flesh." It is

a earth, earthly reality (Ps 24:1);
b humankind as such (Ps 89:12);
c sinful humankind (John 3:16);
d the wrongful order; order as a mask for the forgetfulness of God; that which is valid by default; stupid greed and senseless morality (Matt 13:22; 1 John 2:15).

The world—yes, there we have the letter, the verbal icon, which expresses the extreme opposite of sanctification in the biblical ABCs, especially in the Johannine writings. The world "cannot see Jesus" (John 14:19), the world cannot believe, the world cannot love something other than "its own" (John 15:19). The world is the result of overpowering—the success strategy of the gods and divine powers.

This is very much in opposition to the earth! The earth is called upon to serve YHWH with joy (Ps 100:2); the earth abides forever (Eccl 1:4). The ark, the sign of God's special presence, is called "the ark of the Lord of the whole earth" (Josh 3:11, 13). The "whole earth" is full of God's glory (Isa 6:3), and the "whole earth" will be filled with God's glory (Ps 72:19).

The earth and the sanctuary, the preeminent holy place, do not stand in opposition, but the sanctuary and the *world* do. The seasons of the year and the rite of the temple aren't opposites; neither are human finitude and the holiness of God. Nor are human limitations and sensuality opposed to the holiness that God effects in humans.

One cannot shatter the biblical ABCs more viciously than by presenting it as if the *earth* makes us unholy and resists our sanctification.

Although it is true that we abuse and violate the earth, and also take earth as a hideout and pretext for our loneliness, rebellion, and forgetfulness toward

God, earth itself functions more as a testimony *against* us than as an excuse *for* us. The earth is—primordially—virginal.

The "creation psalms" belong to the sanctuary; in them, the earth is seen through the open windows of the temple—and both are brought to God with never-ending gratitude.

the earth is not profane—

the "world and those living within it" spoil the earth (Ps 24:1); hence the biblical Flood. The shape, form, and "order" of this *world*—*this* world is passing away! (1 Cor 7:31).

This passing away appears on the farthest horizon as the acme of sanctification: as God's last act, the crown of the divine virtues, the fulfillment of the divine word, and the end of God's way. It is the separation of sin from the earth.

> Let sinners vanish *from the earth*,
>   and let the wicked be no more.
> Bless the Lord, O my soul.
> Praise the Lord! (Ps 104:35)

If everything will be sanctified, "each according to its own kind," this means that the "world" will be purified. Then the earth, the original creation, will shine anew from out of the shadow of rebellion, and it will be seen again as the first and final bearer of divine glory.

The "four living creatures" of the book of Revelation, representing the earth that has suffered from disfigurement and exploitation, sing together with the twenty-four elders—the congregation from Israel and the nations—because they are *sanctified* together. They are *one* creation, immersed and uplifted in worship (Rev 5:6).

Whoever sees this vision at a distance also now feels exhorted by creation, by brother sun and sister moon and all the guiltless creatures, to seek their place and find their form of service.

> And in the meantime stood
> on opening horizon
> lucidly ready for a new act
> the diamond dawn.[3]

You make the gateways of the morning and the evening shout for joy (Ps 65:9).

Seek the Lord and live (. . .)
> The one who made the Pleiades and Orion,
> and turns deep darkness into the morning (Amos 5:6, 8)

O Lord, how manifold are your works!
> In wisdom you have made them all;
> the earth is full of your creatures.

May the glory of the Lord endure forever;
> may the Lord rejoice in his works (Ps 104:24, 31)

NOTES

1. Miskotte quotes from J. H. Leopold, a Dutch classicist and poet in the symbolist tradition ("Een lucht van marmer en van onyxsteen," in *Verzen, Fragmenten,* ed. P. N. van Eyck and Johan B. W. Polak, Verzameld Werk, Part 2 [Brusse: Rotterdam/Van Oorschot: Amsterdam, 1951–1952], 313).

2. The word "sabotage" alludes to the writings of the Amsterdam minister Jan Koopmans, who advocated during the war years to renounce antisemitism. He wrote in his 1941 book, *Wat zegt de Bijbel?* [What does the Bible say?]: "We are Christians first, Dutch second" (p. 8), a clear criticism of nationalism and Nazism. A review of his book appeared in a journal published by the Dutch SS, where he was called "a dangerous saboteur."

3. Miskotte quotes here from J.H. Leopold's poem, "In den nacht, als veeg," in *Verzen, Fragmenten*, 433.

Chapter 11

Expectation

1.

On a number of occasions now we have placed before us the *oerwoorden*, or primary words, of Holy Scripture—words that we might not have recognized as such at first glance.

Our sense of surprise at these words probably comes from our all-too-understandable habit of bringing our own primary words to Scripture and using them as a measure for the holy texts. The strange thing is, those primary words of *ours* do not occur at all in Scripture. This is the other side of our surprise. We may of course posit a reasonable explanation for this omission: our words are missing because the Bible was not written by thinkers, but rather by naive souls, on account of which, its worldview and ethos is . . . primitive. And yet this lack of our words in the Bible could have a deeper meaning, and one related closely to the centrality of the "Name."

Which of our words do we mean?

    a *eternity*
    b *all*
    c *nature*
    d *religion*
    e *personality*
    f *virtue*
    g *ideal*

2.

These seven illustrious terms do not appear in the Bible; instead and in their place, other words occur—although the place where a new biblical word occurs is in fact a wholly different place.

a

Scripture speaks of "the age," and of the ages of ages, of the end times, and the life of the age to come. The holy Teaching does not acknowledge a timeless world or even a timeless God.

b

Scripture speaks about "heaven and earth." *Both* are created, *both are no longer* in their original purity; one has been violated through the rebellion of the powers, the other has been violated by human beings. The heavens will "wear out like a garment" (Ps 102:26), there will be "peace in the heavens" (Luke 19:38), and we expect not only a new earth but also new heavens (e.g., Rev 21). The holy Teaching does not acknowledge a closed, self-contained *All*, nor a primordial Life exempted from God's critique.

c

Scripture speaks about the *the whole earth* as the area in which God's acts take place; this same domain is being prepared to be the dwelling place of the Lord. The holy Teaching does not acknowledge an uninterrupted nexus of forces operating according to its own internal laws—what we designate as *nature*.

d

Scripture speaks about the *fear of the Lord* and the service of God in worship and in keeping the commandments; it has much to say about godlessness, straying from God, losing oneself, fornication in the courtyard of the covenant itself. Scripture speaks about answering or not answering God's word. But the holy Teaching does not acknowledge religion as a static condition, nor as a special disposition of the soul, nor as an inner assuredness concerning the peaceable kingdom.

e

Scripture speaks about the human whose *breath is in their nostrils* (Gen 2:7; 17:22), who believes that "their dwellings are on earth forever" (Ps 49:12), and who dies like the animals (Eccl 3:19). The Bible also speaks of the "hidden person of the heart" (1 Pet 3:4, NKJV), who is addressed and unsettled by God's voice. It also says that humans go to their "eternal home," which is the grave (Eccl 12:5). A powerful word on this subject rings out in Pilate's judicial expression, *behold, the man*! (John 19:5). A "man of God" (as in 2 Tim 3:17) is one who is begotten by the Spirit; who belongs to God. But the holy Teaching does not acknowledge "personality" as a mystical and profound dimension of this creature called human; it lacks entirely a vision of some unquenchable spiritual reality, which is, in principle, self-sufficient, developing and unfolding and realizing itself.

f

Scripture speaks about *righteousness* and unrighteousness, meaning right and wrong relationship with God, covenant faithfulness and covenant violation—as well as sometimes about individual "deeds . . . done in God" (John 3:21). The Bible does not acknowledge virtue as an inalienable quality of human nature, which precludes, as if by a higher necessity, certain amoral or immoral actions. No, the holy Teaching does not acknowledge a virtuous person nor a virtuous life, as these are used in either popular discourse or moral philosophy.

g

Scripture speaks about the *commandment* of God, that is, the way by which we stay on the path of God and remain with our Deliverer. It speaks about keeping commandments and breaking them, about statutes and rights. But the keeping of the commandments does not happen with an eye on some ideal to which the godly strive to adhere. Nor does "the imitation of Christ" mean conformity to an ideal. Rather, it indicates a way by which we live in communion with him and accompany him to the cross. "Ideal" does not belong to the biblical *oerwoorden*, primary words, and neither does "virtue," "personality," "religion," "nature," "all," nor "eternity."

3.

What is the deep-seated reason that the Bible outwardly lacks these words that are so dear to us—and inwardly makes no place for them? The reason hangs together with the whole biblical ABCs that we have discussed so far. It relates to the "Name," to the order and the unity of the divine virtues, to the Acts, the Word, the Way, and Sanctification. But, if we discern rightly, this omission and rejection of our *oerwoorden* has the most direct connection with *expectation*: a biblical word to which we will dedicate our attention in order to provisionally conclude our instruction in the ABCs.

If there were no other reasons—but they are plentiful—the biblical word "expectation" would in itself suffice completely to *undermine* the aforementioned *grondwoorden* or ground-words that we bring with us, and to expose them as *idols*. To put it simply, and in terms of these rejected words themselves (though this is admittedly not a pure line of reasoning since these words cannot apply at all), "expectation" entails that: there is not yet any "eternity." There is not yet a "universe" or "all." There is not yet any "nature." There is not yet any religion, or personality, or virtue, or ideal. Said otherwise: if these words were to be regarded as human articulations of the truth (which is not the case), then they would be unmasked as speculative, premature, arbitrary, and obstinate through the holy Teaching's *continual* speech about "expectation." It seems as if *this* letter of the biblical ABCs contains a critical force that constantly prevents the growth of our human ideas and dreams. This power imparts itself to all the biblical verbs that describe the life of humans. Just think of this odd biblical term: *to walk* (Gen 5:22, 24; 17:1; Lev 26:12, 41; Deut 1:30, 33; 28:9; 1 Kgs 9:4; Ps 81:14; 101:6; Prov 6:22; 14:16; Eph 2:10; 1 John 2:6).

Why this usage of the rather naive verb "to walk," which seems to us either pre-religious or post-religious? Either paradisal or a bourgeois inanity? The answer is:

> "It has not yet been revealed what we shall be" (1 John 3:2, NKJV)—not as a worldly reality, a public event, nor a decisive world order. Throughout the entire Old and New Testaments, the bells of Advent are sounding.

Hear, for example, Micah 4:1–5 (NRSV, adapt.):

> In days to come
>   the mountain of the Lord's house
> shall be established as the head of the mountains,
>   and shall be raised up above the hills.
> Peoples shall stream to it,
>   and many nations shall come and say:
> "Come, let us go up to the mountain of the Lord,
>   to the house of the God of Jacob;
> that he may teach us his ways
>   and that we may walk in his paths."
> (. . .)
>   He shall judge between many peoples,

and shall arbitrate between strong nations far away;
they shall beat their swords into plowshares,
    and their spears into pruning hooks;
nation shall not lift up sword against nation,
    neither shall they learn war any more;
 but they shall all sit under their own vines and under their own fig trees,
    and no one shall make them afraid;
    for the mouth of the Lord of Hosts has spoken.
 The nations may walk for now
each in the name of their own gods
But we will walk in the name of the Lord our God
forever and ever.

This is just one passage; but who among you cannot think immediately of many more? As further examples: Isa 2:1ff; 9:5f; 11:1–9; 25:6ff; 32:15–17; Ps 72:17. Or again, Ps 85:10–11, where it is written:

Steadfast love and faithfulness will meet;
    righteousness and peace will kiss each other.
Faithfulness will spring up from the ground,
    and righteousness will look down from the sky.

Such is also the sense of the biblical stories of patriarchs, judges, and kings after God's own heart: they let *expectation* shine through in every one of their failures and accomplishments.

4.

This much is actually rather obvious; it is grounded in the structure of the biblical message as anti-pagan testimony (*anti!*—but we now know how laden this negative designation is with positive power: with liberation, exaltation, and salvation). For the following is sure:

PAGANISM HAS NO EXPECTATION,

because it does not acknowledge time as purposeful; because it does not discern the Way. That is why it knows how to deal with the remnants of expectation that have remained in the human soul. These are destroyed, thrown into the abyss of the Existent. The tiny pieces are swept under the carpet, and the larger ones are, with more or less ceremonial gesturing, cremated. There is no purpose (for that is "naive"). We are not going anywhere (for that is a childish wish, to go somewhere). We are in motion and yet at a standstill; such is the meaning of resignation—"at ease!"

Why is purposelessness like this thinkable? Because there is no *Middle of time*; or in other words, because the "Name" is not known. If we had not known them yet, the consequences here are as palpable as if we grasped them by hand: the consequence of humans wanting to know about Deity but not about YHWH; or about *in*finity but not about meeting God; or about an abstract "Omnipotence," but not about the virtues of this singular God, who has "established a memorial" for the divine Name upon the earth (Exod 3:15). Where no Middle of time exists, *neither a beginning nor an ending* is thinkable, and we live unbounded, with neither left nor right, neither above nor below, neither good nor evil. This unbounded or boundaryless condition is home to limitless freedom—and also immeasurable loneliness. Everything is, in such a place, just as weighty, or, which amounts to the same, just as weightless. No true form or actual decision is possible in the boundless realm of Primordial Material, of *tohu* Chaos, of *Ginnungagap* (of Germanic myth). What is decisive: in the limitless realm there is neither

a real past nor a real future.

See! So much depends on Revelation; on the Name; on Jesus Christ; on the Middle of Time, and on the divine inbreaking into all that we have built to camouflage the unbounded abyss: the complete All, the self-contained nexus of nature, the silence of eternity, the mysticism of religion in which we see ourselves as our "self," the inextinguishable personality, virtue, and ideal. Such *images* became indispensable to us, since we were damned to look upon the Limitless, but found that we could not. Unboundedness—it is the delusion of our heritage, which knows full well that it is a delusion; hence the tenacity of modern paganism.

Unboundedness—in comparison with life under the Name, it offers not one step toward an enlarged existence. It merely seals the essential loneliness, lostness, and abandon of our souls. The unbounded exposes our soul like a foundling, and thought itself is rendered defenseless.

5.

The first and last word of Scripture is: expectation. After all, the *creation story* is ordered such that it climaxes with the *Sabbath*, and the Sabbath, together with the Sabbatical year and the year of Jubilee, acknowledges and proclaims that God, *this* God, wills and works for the peace of the world. God works where we rest; we must know that, whatever the value of our work may be, it cannot and must not seek to contribute to the miracle of the End Time, the creation of the divine order called the "Reign" or "Kingdom" of God. Such is the beginning of the "narrative philosophy" of Scripture.[1] And it ends with this cry that rings out through heaven and earth: Come, Lord Jesus, come soon (Rev 22:20).

So we should certainly not see expectation as a mere appendix to the teaching, an afterthought of praxis; it is much more so a qualification that stamps all words of Scripture without exception. Creation! Creation happened *for the sake of* the End, of *this* End. Covenant! There must be a people "who offer themselves willingly on the day of your power" (Ps 110:3, NRSV adapt.). Second birth! We have been born again into a living *hope* through the resurrection of Jesus Christ from the dead (1 Pet 1:3). And the signs that seemed to have done their service in the past, return as signs of the future. (This sequence corresponds to what we heard earlier about the way in which the unity of Scripture obtains: first the Old, then the New, and then the Old Testament again). The Messiah *has* come, but he is "coming again," in his Future. The Kingdom (Ps 2:6; Luke 17:21; Rev 12:10); Jerusalem (Ps 122; Gal 4:26; Heb 12:22; Rev 3:12; 21:2, 10); Zion (Ps 48:3; Zech 9:9; Ps 87:5; Rev 14:1); the tabernacle (Exod 40:34; John 1:14) (he tabernacled among us); John 2:21 (the temple of his body); Rev 21:3: "See, the tabernacle of God is among mortals"; the manna (Exod 16:35; John 6:33; Rev 2:17). See, each one returns; the signs

RETURN AS SIGNS OF THE FUTURE,

for the promises are fulfilled and—no, there is still a part to fulfill! *The* peace has not yet arrived, neither in the world nor in our heart.

What we have received of peace is a pledge of that which is still Coming, which draws near.

Reconciliation is complete, but redemption is still outstanding. The second Coming makes public what was hidden.

Even Creation itself in the beginning, which we can no longer access in some unmediated way in "nature"—even Creation must still be revealed. The beauty of the Creator in the Creation, or as the Bible says, God's glory, is a *future* world for us. But the glimmer of light that we already witness is a sufficient sign and pledge of our expectation.

Let us read Romans 8:19 and follow with a new receptivity:

> For the creation waits with eager *expectation* for the revealing of the children of God; for the creation was subjected to futility, not of its own will but by the will of the one who subjected it, *in hope* that the creation itself will be set free from its bondage to decay and will obtain the freedom of the glory of the children of God. (. . .) but we ourselves, who have the first fruits of the Spirit, groan inwardly while we *wait* for adoption, the redemption of our bodies. For in hope

we were saved. Now hope that is seen is not hope. For who hopes for what is seen? But if we hope for what we do not see, we wait for it with patience.

We hear a hidden sorrow living within this proclamation, but we hear also its saturation with that attitude that can be called preeminently "biblical": the certainty, which, as the certainty of the Name, is incomparably certain.

Expectation belongs to this God and to the Name. Only if this God is the Deity, if YHWH is Elohim and El Shaddai and El Sebaoth and our Father—only then does expectation make sense; and only by virtue of this Revelation and by dwelling in the holy Teaching as in one's own world will it be possible to persevere in this expectation in spite of ourselves.

6.

Just as "sanctification" permeates all the forms and shapes of holy Teaching, and no thing or action or condition can be imagined that is not governed by the meaning of this *verb*, in the same way, "expectation" so qualifies and characterizes the movement of the human heart that without it one is left futile, corrupted, or even completely worthless. And then of course, it turns out that the *human being* is revealed as unconscious, corrupted, worthless, if the human being lacks expectation. The qualification "sanctification" contains indeed a qualifying condition: sanctification is *for* expectation, that is to say, it prepares its recipient for a life-of-hope that would otherwise be impossible for our nature.

Expectation belongs inseparably to humans who are being "sanctified." Only if it is God who has set us apart and unsettled us does expectation have a firm foundation.

Only if the "flesh" does not belong to the original nature, and if it is not a substance but misdirection of the will, can there be any hope, for Adam and all his offspring.

Only when the Spirit overcomes the flesh do the old begin to dream dreams and the young to see visions (Acts 2:17; Joel 2:28).

The dream! the DREAM!

No, it will always be characteristic of the "flesh," which is to say, for "fallen" humanity, for natural religion, for reason, society, for the "world," that it does not dream like the prophets do, both before and after Pentecost. And, conversely, the sanctification of all things can be understood as the ordering and alignment of human life on the *pre*supposition of *final* expectation.

Whatever the sanctified human does, it remains dubious, half-hearted, dull, a bare form, an abortive attempt, unless all their works are driven out and shapen by the *verb: to expect.*

SEE, THE WORK WITHIN ALL WORKS!

Believing and praying and serving, sowing and mowing and harvesting, cult, culture and nature, struggle, suffering, and endurance—in Scripture they are, while maintaining their own value and integrity, manifestations of the one work, which is: man-work; dreamwork; bride-work, child-work.

> The work of prophets, priests and kings,
> the work of the "Remnant that repents,"
> the work of the servants that wait for their Lord,
> the work of the lonely one who looked forward to the consolation of Israel (Luke 2:25),
> the work within all works, *the* human response to sanctification, *the* talent, *the* power of faith;
> the pure praying contained within prayer,
> the secret motion in every movement of sowing,
> the actual driving force in our becoming,
> the purest meaning in our act of love,
> the blessedness of "the poor in spirit."

No wonder; even understood as charitably as possible, what was meant by eternity, all, nature, religion, personality, virtue, ideal *does not exist*. Rather, it *comes*! We don't *have* it in possession; we *expect* it. And, far from having nothing in the dream, we find in it everything that there is to find during this between-time. In the meantime, a form of worship and a culture are born that owe their existence and right to exist to no other force than the awakening power of this expectation.

6a.

Let us hear this now:

> Do not let those who wait for you be put to shame . . .
> for you I wait all day long . . .
> May integrity and uprightness preserve me,
>   for I wait for you (Ps 25:3, 5, 21).

I *wait* for your salvation, O Lord (Gen 49:18).

Wait for the Lord;
> be strong, and let your heart take courage;
> *wait* for the Lord! (Ps 27:14).

Even youths will faint and be weary,
> and the young will fall exhausted;

but those who wait for the Lord shall renew their strength,
> they shall mount up with wings like eagles,

they shall run and not be weary,
> they shall walk and not faint (Isa 40:30–31).

It is from there that we are expecting a Savior, the Lord Jesus Christ. He will transform the body of our humiliation that it may be conformed to the body of his glory, by the power that also enables him to make all things subject to himself (Phil 3:20b–21).

The Lord is good to those who wait for him (Lam 3:25).

For he looked forward to the city that has foundations, whose architect and builder is God (Heb 11:10).

But, in accordance with his promise, we wait for new heavens and a new earth, where righteousness is at home (2 Pet 3:13).

For the needy shall not always be forgotten,
> nor the hope of the poor perish forever (Ps 9:18).

For surely I know the plans I have for you, says the Lord, plans for your welfare and not for harm, to give you a future with hope (Jer 29:11).

O Lord, you, Israel's EXPECTATION,
> its savior in time of trouble!

Why should you be like a stranger in the land,
> like a traveler turning aside for the night?

Why should you be like someone confused,
> like a mighty warrior who cannot give help?

Yet you, O Lord, are in the midst of us,
> and we are called by your Name;
> do not forsake us! (Jer 14:8–9, NRSV adapt.)

And in the New Testament we read:

Let us hold fast to the confession of our hope without wavering, for he who has promised is faithful (Heb 10:23).

and for a helmet the hope of salvation (1 Thess 5:8);
Christ Jesus *our hope* (1 Tim 1:1).

7.

If we ask about the content of expectation, the answer must be none other than God or the Kingdom or a sign of the Kingdom.

"I wait for *you*—you yourself. You are not present now, and I experience your absence; I miss your special presence." It is necessary, in one way or another, to wait for a

Coming into presence.

This Coming applies to matters small and great, to the personal and suprapersonal, to the people of God and the *goyim*, the church and the state, humanity and nature. For all, a coming is necessary. Do you now understand, you student of the ABCs, what an immense distance gapes between the teaching of Scripture and the teachings of religion?

Consolation does not well up from ourselves, but it comes from without.

Help is not recruited by us, but it comes.

Reconciliation is not our discovery of our own delusion and alienation; it is *effected* for us.

Promise is not our wish; it is sent to us.

God is come into the camp! (1 Sam 4:7).
for he is *coming*, for he is *coming* to judge the earth (Ps 96:13; 98:9; 1 Chr 16:33).
Our God comes and does not keep silence . . . Out of Zion, the perfection of beauty,
God *shines forth* (Ps 50:3, 2)
I lift up my eyes to the hills—
from where will my help come? (Ps 121:1)
I saw one like a human being
coming with the clouds of heaven (Dan 7:13).
Lo, your king comes to you; humble (Zech 9:9).

Behold, THE DAYS ARE COMING.

And therefore: *Sentinel, what of the night?* (Isa 21:11) (You see, whereas doubt is not biblical, *questioning* itself is biblical—questioning empowered by expectation: the question of right timing, the question of embarrassment over delay, the question of prophetic and apostolic and once again prophetic hearts)

> For the Son of Man *came* to seek out and to save the lost (Luke 19:10).
> He came to what was his own, and his own did not accept him (John 1:11).
> But you will receive power when the Holy Spirit has come upon you (Acts 1:8).
> Your kingdom COME (Matt 6:10).

The verb *to visit* also means: to wait, expect, come, appear, in a living context, whether hidden or public (Exod 4:31; 13:19; Ruth 1:6; 1 Sam 2:21; Ps 8:5; 65:10; 106:4: "O Lord, visit me with your salvation"; Zech 10:3: "the Lord will visit his flock"; Luke 1:78: "Through the tender mercy of our God, with which the Dayspring from on high has *visited* us" [NKJV]; Luke 7:16: "a great prophet has risen up among us, and God has visited his people.")

8.

To the question of what we may expect, another answer can be: either the Messiah or the Messianic Kingdom.

Messianic *expectation* is to be distinguished from messianic desire. The first is assured a priori by virtue of the Name, the Middle of time. The fulfillment that *has* already come in the first appearance of the Messiah also legitimates and fills up the promise to the full.

And then we consider the salvation and setting right of all that *inferior matter*, which idealism and spiritualized paganism detest: the fire upon the earth, which is to say, its purification; the gathering of nations, the resurrection of the flesh, and the glorification of creation. What a vulgar undertaking, yes? At least according to the taste of Platonists! We say, what realism! in the face of all dreams of ruin, extinction, submersion, evaporation, or dissolution into the divine. This latter is, unbeknownst, the very highest ambition of natural religion. But the Bible takes an extremely realistic approach.

This is why earthly things in the Bible are treated so intensely, so weightily; there is a fragrance of promise over the entire world, over the body, and over human labor. The Bible also knows about "vanity," the emptiness and futility of life. But this vanity is not intrinsic to creation. It is the negativity, the lostness of human life, which indeed stares us in the face from the mirror of nature.

There is no more biblical word for the experience of negativity in life than the term *shame*, and *becoming ashamed*. There is no plea more desperate than the plea: "let me not be ashamed." And there is no promise more poignant than the promise: "whoever believes in him will not be put to shame" (Ezra 9:6; Ps 22:6; 25:3; 69:7; Isa 24:23; 26:11; Jer 20:11; 2 Cor 9:4; 10:8; Phil 1:20; 1 Pet 2:6; 3:16; Ps 40:15; 70:3; Isa 50:7; 1 Pet 4:16).

Whoever experiences shame apparently expects something different than what we have been trained to expect; they have built expectation on grounds other than the Name, or set hope on powers other than those revealed in the Virtues of God, or labored on endeavors besides those that align with the Way.

As a result of mislaying expectation, or of denying expectation, a person

SUFFERS SHAME.

Or—a possibility that really occupied the pious of old age—even good expectation can incur shame! The affliction that reverberates throughout the books of *Job* and *Ecclesiastes* and Psalm 73 is the suffering of shame and disgrace. Had no promise been given and no expectation awakened, if no trust were born in the soul, then Job's truculence, Ecclesiastes's sullenness, and Asaph's complaint would not have taken on such immense dimensions. Divine "proving" or testing and many other secrets of salvation have long lain hidden in this ashamedness. We will explore this topic no further; it will suffice to see the spiritual complementarity of expectation and shame.

8a.

The inverse of complete expectation is the experience of total shame. Such is the inheritance of the pagans and those who violate the covenant. Hear, for example, Zephaniah 1:14–18:

> The great day of the Lord is near,
>   near and hastening fast;
> the sound of the day of the Lord is bitter,
>   He thunders, the Hero—
> That day is the day of boundlessness
> A day of fear and anguish
> A day of devastation and whirlwind
> A day of clouds and thunder-darkness,
> A day of trumpet and blasting sound
> against the fortified cities
>   against the high-rising towers.
> I will bring fear to the people
> They will walk away like the blind
> On the day of *his* boundlessness

In the fire of his passion
He will make an end,
An end to all the cultivators, all the tenants
Of this world.[2]

9.

Now, in biblical speech, the "minor" expectation opens onto the "major" expectation; the "small" help is a pledge of the greater pledge, the "small" consolation anticipates eternal consolation. The "little" appearances herald the final Coming. Hence the special emphasis and the particular weight placed on the word

SIGN

in the biblical ABCs; in the spiritual grammar of Scriptures; and in the context of the holy Teaching.

Expectation, the action of expecting, may be strengthened by signs, which is to say, by those realities that *point to* the last reality, and those acts that are a pledge of divine Kingship. "YHWH appointed a sign for Cain, so that no one finding him would slay him" (Gen 4:15, NASB). "The rainbow is given as a sign of the covenant between God and the earth" (Gen 9:12, 13, 17).

Of circumcision it is written: "and that will be a sign of the covenant between me and between you" (Gen 17:11).

Miracles themselves are just as many signs of the acts of the Lord; of the Way and the promise of God's future (Josh 24:17; 1 Sam 10:7; Isa 38:7; Ps 78:43).

> Therefore the Lord himself will give you a sign. Look, the young woman is with child and shall bear a son, and shall name him Immanuel (Isa 7:14).

> What will be the sign of your coming? (Matt 24:3, NKJV).

> God confirmed the word by signs that followed (Mark 16:20).

Even though the Egyptian magicians also perform great signs; even though it is said: "The evil and adulterous generation requests a sign"; even though Simon the Sorcerer is astonished at the signs that the apostles performed and wanted to buy the Pneuma, the power to perform in the same way (Acts 8:13)—for there are false signs as well as erroneous use of true ones—nevertheless, the sign remains: as a seal of the acts of God and as a guarantee of expectation. We cannot remove these two aspects from one another. Signs console and accompany the people of God, the church.

Here again we consider the seriousness of godliness, which lives from both biblical testaments, in the unity of what has already been fulfilled and the fulfillment that is still coming. Abraham saw Christ's day (John 8:56). And *we* see in Abraham a sign of the way that leads from the first to the second Coming; he is the father of all believers (Rom 4:11).

For the New Testament congregation, the whole of the Old Testament history is a sign, *because* the people of the Old Testament considered it a sign of what was, for them, still coming.

There are no "Middle Ages" that the new age supplants. Because the new history begins in Christ, it brings all of world history into the light and shows that it was the "Middle Ages," the Dark Age, all along. Since we live in this dispensation of the "middle" period, the power of these actions endures: working and praying, lamenting and singing, dying and exulting. All the secret deeds of the soul retain their propulsive force: believing, hoping, attaching oneself and detaching oneself, wanting-to-be-young, wanting-to-grow-old, maturing. The power of expectation matures; it is the desire to be betrothed to the Messiah through his promise and our confession.

As

A WEDDING RING

the Messiah has given us the *sign*, though its form differs depending on its particular recipient, whether that is the earth, humanity, Israel, the church, or a single soul. If here and there the form of the sign changes, its status as a sign does not: circumcision, for example, functioned in Israel as a sign of the covenant, and it is still a sign of the Name for us newcomers to the covenant.

"For our paschal lamb, Christ, has been sacrificed" (1 Cor 5:7)—this is a different sign from the first Passover lamb. At the same time, by this other, new sign, we "proclaim the Lord's death until he comes" (1 Cor 11:26), which is to say, with an eye on his future.

Because the people of the New Testament live in expectation, the church should experience not only the coherence but the unity of the two testaments. It is not only the *oerwoorden* or primary words like creation, sanctification, covenant, faith, promise, and commandment that make the New Testament an Israelite book and a witness to the one, divine Name. It is also the world-of-signs, the sacramental space, in which things and persons, names and symbols, are placed. For in remembrance or in expectation, these signs contribute to the *communal* good both in Israel and in the church. This observation applies to all the vocabulary of the Old Testament: the meaning of its *oerwoorden* is not exhausted by their fulfillment *there*, and neither is it exhausted *here*:

"day" and "light," "pillar of fire" and "manna," "temple," "gold," *shalom* or "peace" that includes both inner well-being and outer prosperity, the "arm," "hand," "finger," and "face" of God—they were known in their reality at that time. But their reality as such called in turn for . . . expectation!

Signs address *humble* human beings, who know that they live between the times. The proud demand all or nothing. But in truth, "all or nothing" is always an evasion: such persons want to overcome faith and therefore they despise signs, which are a seal of truth and also show the provisionality of revelation. We must understand the words of the Old Testament in this way: as a restless shuttling back and forth of thought, from promise to fulfillment and then to promise again: shadow and reality, and reality that is itself only a shadow of what is yet to come.

Thus *people*, God's people, return as a *sign* of the second coming, just as the first people of God, Israel, were a sign of the first coming. The church! The signs of God's calling and election are established in its midst, and it has itself become a sign: all its faults are manifest (just like Israel), but its true identity is hidden in God, and it participates hiddenly in all the treasures and benefits of Christ, and it will be revealed in glory in God's future (Matt 1:21; 2:6; 21:43; Luke 2:10; Rom 9:25f; Heb 8:10; 2 Cor 6:16; Heb 13:12; 1 Pet 2:9f; Rev 18:4; 21:3).

Or consider a biblical word like "life." "*Life*" occurs throughout the Scriptures, and it indicates the accumulation of forces, set within the irreversible linearity of time. Life is always real, and yet still not real enough, but "only" a premonition, foretaste, in short, a sign of . . . *eternal* life (Gen 19:17; Prov 8:35; John 1:4; Ps 72:15; John 10:28; Isa 38:19; John 14:19). It would be a *lie* if desire would forget what it already possesses; but it would amount to *death* if the possessor did not know how to desire more.

10.

The word that marks the highest, deepest, and nearest object of expectation, that identifies the salvation standing by the door, is

GLORY.

The Teaching makes us know the Name; within the Name lies the revelation of all God's virtues; under the dominion of the Name we are sanctified; sanctification happens to strengthen expectation; expectation holds fast to the signs; and signs prefigure the revelation of Glory, the *eternal* Glory.

Now we must be careful at the end of our discourse not to abandon this biblical trend-line and to break out of the particular frame of the ABCs—by falling back on our *human concept of "eternity"* as endlessly extended time or as a standstill of timeless being. We do not first have a concept of "eternity" that we then apply to God and say, God is eternal, just as we cannot apply our a priori concept of "God" to YHWH. *No, God's self is eternity*, in the same way as God's self must be called love, justice, mercy, patience, the word, the light, the power, the omnipotence. God is not untouched by what we call "time," and therefore *this* eternity, which is the eternity of *this* God, is not a contradiction to time.

God is the One *who is and who was and who is to come* (Rev 1:4, 8; 4:8; 11:17). That is God's essence and that is God's eternity. In the same way that God is Father, Son, and Spirit, God is in God's own self what was and is and is to come. Because God is eternally the Father, eternally the Son, eternally the Spirit, and lives thus as the eternal God. And this One has in Jesus Christ *assumed time* as the form and shape of God's eternal being.

God gives us time, and God has time for us. God acts, and these acts stem from God's eternity in the space of our time. *God exists together with us in one and the same life.* God walks a Way with us such that, throughout all times, God does not suffer loss, but rather takes time up and accepts it into union with the divine self.

The non-biblical idea of God's immutability means that God is Death; and in the same way, the non-biblical idea of God's Omnipotence means that God is a Demon. So, too, with the non-biblical idea of God's eternity: it means that God is Nothingness, the Ab-solute (the ultimate loosening from us), the Abyss, the Void.

Let us, rather, hear the murmur of life in this holy triad of God's eternal being and work:

WHO IS
WHO WAS
WHO IS TO COME

The Living One is God; the one who does not negate time but takes it up—that one is God. The one who is merciful and righteous, patient and faithful, is God. The one who travels on the Way, who creates history, holy history, who judges and saves, who intersects and encloses world history.

God is above time, and also before and after it. This we confess because God has come *in* time, or rather, because time is taken up into God through Jesus Christ our Lord.

In connection with expectation, what is said above requires this particular emphasis: God has and God is that which we are not yet and which we do not yet have. God thus *transcends* time, in that God lives before and after time, as the Beginning and the End, the Alpha and the Omega, the First and the Last

(Rev 1:11; 21:6; 22:13; Isa 41:4; 44:6; 48:12). We do not seek a careful balance with this *oerwoord* or primary word, because we are not writing a dogmatic theology, but this is not the only reason. Such a balance does not exist in the Bible itself, either; and this cannot possibly be otherwise, for we are sanctified *toward* expectation. The hope of glory *remains*. God will most truly be our God in the next aeon, in the revelation of God's eternal *beauty*. We draw ever nearer to that day, and we look forward to it in this poor, ravaged life.

11.

The Glory of God is God's eternal, or so to say, latent power to reveal the divine self as it is, in the midst and over against the rule of gods and demons.

Glory is the Revelation in and above all revelations, ready to break forth and triumph over all that we know: matter and spirit, good and evil, past and present and future.

The Glory *is coming*; but it can only *arrive*, because it *is* in God, and it lives and works—because YHWH lives, thinks, and acts in and from out of Glory.

There are no words for this! Of course there are no words for it. For Glory has no separate content of its own, it is the coherence of all God's actions, the *harmony* of all divine virtues, the meaning of God's way. "How beautiful God must be!"

We can draw an analogy: there are no words to describe the Glory, just as words fail in describing the beauty of a work of art. One can admire the material, the concept, the unity, the perspective, the meaning, the purpose. But what *is* it actually? What does it *say*? What should we *do* with it? After critical scrutiny, deliberation and evaluation and appreciation, nothing remains to say except: beautiful! precious! magnificent!

It IS
It is IT!

12.

What remains then except—to *sing*, which is a glorified speaking, a speaking in which speaking is enhanced, lifted up, and in this way, justified and sanctified. That is why the Bible is full of singing. The angels are creatures of song; and the elect, the people of God, the church—within the temple, in their deepest humility, they know nothing better than a psalm, a song, a hymn; with the sounding of the trumpet, with lute and harp, with string instruments and organ, with shrill sounding cymbals, with cymbals of joy (Ps 150). Therefore, the Bible says that *life itself* in heaven will be—*singing*.

And they sang a new song:

> You are worthy to take the scroll containing the Counsel of God, O Christ, Lamb of God, and to open its seals . . . and I looked and I heard the voice of many angels surrounding the throne and the living creatures (the living earth) and the elders (the living congregation) and they numbered myriads of myriads and thousands of thousands, saying: "You are worthy to receive power and wealth and wisdom and might and honor and glory and thanksgiving" (Rev 5:9, 11–12, NRSV adapt.).

Would there be any reason to sing the Samsara, the cycle of births (according to Buddhism)? What could we possibly sing in Nirvana? Or in the apprehension of the *Götterdämmerung*, the twilight of the gods? Or under the pressure of the *Schicksal* (Fate)? Or how could we be provoked to sing before the "gods of this age"?

Bead after glistening bead hangs in its strict sequence along the sacred cord of *oerwoorden*, the primary biblical words: *this* God is the Deity, this Name is given to us; there is no other name under heaven by which we must be saved. *This* God, who unfolds the divine Virtues in the unity of Love, in the unity of God's freely-willed mercy—this God effects the divine Acts, sends forth the divine Word, walks the divine Way. This One is glorious, reveals divine Glory, and gives us to *share* in that Glory. The world will be bright because of God's light, which dwells eternally in the deeps of God. Joy will become manifest through the power of God's own unending jubilation, by which God lives within and alongside God's own self.

12a.

This *verb* lights up within the series of biblical *oerwoorden*:

TO EXULT,

namely, now: in the midst of misery and hardship, when one encounters the *signs*, and especially when the divine "*Face*" or special presence visits us.

At such times, mere reverence (fear of the Lord) does not suffice, and neither does admiration nor gratitude, let alone acquiescence, submission, duty, or obedience. Instead what arises is: delight, joy, pleasure, praise, glorification, *exultation*. The enthronement psalms are full of it (Pss 93–99)!

Exultation is an *anticipation* of the *consummation*: a placing of oneself already in the Day of Days.

This work waits for us along the long road of expectation, here and there; it lies wherever the signs are, in the service of Worship, and before the divine Face. It stretches itself out toward the Future, it is possible because of the future, since it consists in rays of Glory thrown backward ahead of time—but it takes place *here* and *now*, regardless of reality as we consider it and in spite of our *sin and guilt* and in the face of Satan. It outpaces all the fury of demons and the raging of the nations, all the tears of the oppressed and the day of vengeance. It occurs in divine self-forgetfulness. But we are beginning to preach, and such is not the intention of this discourse; we can merely indicate these things, for we must keep our focus formal and learn only to read the holy Teaching. And yet shouldn't attention to the form press us beyond the formal, especially when the form itself is irregular—when we elaborate on glory, should not our discourse give way to . . . singing? Nevertheless, let us return to our theme, whose material content the form of the biblical ABCs presents to us, and let us listen to the tune of some Bible texts.

> Let all who take refuge in you rejoice, for ever and ever;
> Let them sing for joy, because you spread your protection over them,
> Let those who love your name, *exult* you (Ps 5:11, NRSV adapt.).

> May we shout for joy over your salvation and in the name of *our* God set up our banners (Ps 20:5, NRSV adapt.).

> O come, let us sing to the *Lord*;
>   let us make a joyful noise to the rock of our salvation (= liberation, freedom)!
> Let us come before his Face with thanksgiving;
>   let us make a joyful noise to him with songs of praise!
> (Ps 95:1, NRSV adapt.)

Let us remind ourselves that even lifeless things and unknowing beings are called to exult, and they participate in jubilation; the mountains and trees, the fields of wheat, heaven and earth, the Gentiles, the poor, the mute (Ps 100:1; Isa 35:2; 44:23 [shout for joy, O depths of the earth]; 49:13; Jer 51:48; Isa 35:6 [the tongue of the speechless sings for joy]; Ps 65:14; 67:5). These passages indicate to us that just as these creatures do not exult in a literal sense, so, too, even in the new world, on the new earth and the new heavens, exultation is in essence and first of all a spiritual movement. This is so even as we do well to envision divine glory and our participation in it fully and concretely, humanly, indeed, as a glorification of our humanity.

13.

Instead of speaking of "Glory," we might also have spoken of the *Kingdom* as the destination of God's way and the endpoint of expectation for those who are sanctified. The Kingdom signifies the "Glory" under the viewpoint of *dominion, government, regulation*, the *living together* of God and human, angels and humans, humans and humans. It is about righteousness, about peace, about kindred. We can also say: it is about the fulfillment of the commandments, the establishment of God's Law, the revelation of God's Honor, the effulgence of divine virtues in the mutual relationship of creatures; or: it is about childhood, solidarity, and service, about understanding and respect for each other.

Yet, we think, it is better to conclude with the expectation of Glory, because it aligns better with the holy Teaching to illuminate the Kingdom from the perspective of Glory than the other way around, namely, to consider Glory from the perspective of the Kingdom. Besides, the *same distinctions and stipulations* apply to the Kingdom as they did to Glory. The Kingdom, too, is both in the future and at the same time, close by. It has specific occasions or moments. It grows, *and* it will decisively come. The signs of the Kingdom are augurs of the Messiah, in his miracles, in the *church* that is the community of saints, in the "advancement of the word" (Acts 12:24), in the blessing that is the sacraments, in the working of the apostolate, in deeds of love.

This much is certain: only as the reverse side of Glory is the Kingdom glorious among creatures. Our natural, gullible heart asks endlessly, "is it really true?" or: "how can these things be?" Notice that in the Bible, *Truth* is always connected with promise, and with faithfulness to promise. "God will never break God's truth, God's covenant."[3] In many places, Truth is almost synonymous with glory. What do we expect, when we wait for the resurrection, the new earth, the Kingdom, and the Glory?

We may state an answer negatively. Expectation authenticates our *unbelief* (as God taught us). We see the untruth, the nullity, the impermanence of the gods. Even in that limit situation and in that unimaginable judgment, it will be a clash of *power against power*. God will act, decisively. "As the lightning lights up from one end of heaven to another, radiating under the heavens, so shall the Son of man be in his Day" (Luke 17:24). Whether it is night or mist, lightning reveals the default, given reality as unreal and shows glory as the one and only reality.

Truth—a very important biblical word, about which we cannot, unfortunately, speak—triumphs, and this triumph is the revelation of that which was hidden, namely, the Name, the Revelation: the divine covenant faithfulness and the constancy of divine promise; the reality that silently, constantly surrounds us, and yet also rushes upon us in discrete, divine acts, which will reach their terminus in the last act of the End Times.

Today *Truth* = the efficacy of the divine Redeemer, which we experience at firsthand. Truth also *now* towers over reality; this is already implicitly said by the *Name*. So Truth is . . . God? No, God is Truth! God's Love, the unity of virtues, is the Truth that abides and will be manifest on the Day of Days.

14.

If we live with the kind of insight, vision, and expectation we have been discussing, then we will understand that these very things send us out into life; into our place, our position, our mission. Where does the Word of God meet us? In life! And where does it *want us to go*? Surely not to an edifying meeting, a cloister, a small group, a tea or coffee party, an ivory tower, or a "spiritual life" that runs parallel to human life? Human life is exactly what Jesus Christ once and for all assumed and accepted! So, too, the reflection of Truth, just as with the pledge of love, finds humans nowhere else than in their creaturely place, in their life as given, their determinate lot, their daily vocation and struggle.

The Name, the Virtues, the Acts of God, the Truth, inexorably excludes isolated spirituality and overwrought piety. We expect the revelation of God nowhere else than in life, on this earth, now and always.

Truth is the working and faith-keeping of God, who is the *Lord* of our *reality*, and who will be revealed as such.

The glory of the Kingdom will prove to be the truth of creation; of God's way and of God's counsel. We are bewildered by the world.

That is why the high points of the Bible culminate in the *oath* of God: God's oath taken on the divine self—and equivalent, oath-like expressions.

Verily, verily, I say unto you . . .

TruJly!

Truly in the Lord our God
   is the salvation of Israel (Jer 3:23).

"Truly this man was God's Son!" (Mark 15:39).

The Lord is truly risen (Luke 24:34, NRSV, adapt.).

They will declare, "God is truly among you" (1 Cor 14:25).

I will surely bless you and multiply you (Heb 6:14).

Listen to the Word, not as a human word but as what it really is, God's Word (1 Thess 2:13).

Earnest expectation makes sense only if these words are truly God's words, if the Name is truly revelation, if Jesus Christ is truly God's Son and has risen truly—if God is truly good and

GLORIOUS in GOD'S OWN SELF.

Da Costa's language and tone is biblical when he sings:

At the end post of the times
Our eye meets the spirit of Evil
Too tired to struggle and unarmed
Not capable of another attack.

If the Lord God in all
And in all will be everything
It will be light
eternal light it will be
Light!
From light and darkness![4]

When that day comes and the shadows flee, then the miracle, the new creation, will be in substance nothing more than the unfolding of the *Name*, which already now establishes the memory of God on the earth; then before every eye and every mind, the Lord will be separated from all that is called god—"in that day the Lord will be one and his Name one" (Zech 14:9); then all images will flow into the truth, and the world and we ourselves, too, will spotlessly reflect the Virtues of God. In the same way that we must *learn to live* by considering death and what awaits beyond its limits, and so to live before God's Face, starting today—thus also, we will learn from this messianic future to endure the events of the world, to discern them and take them up into our priestly intercession.

We know *everything* about death, and also *nothing* about it: everything, since the knowledge of death contains all that is necessary to understand life—and nothing, in that we ourselves have not yet died. In the same way, we know everything and also nothing about heaven. We know everything necessary, because we know God in this life; we know nothing insofar as we are not in heaven. Similarly, we know everything and nothing about the Glory: everything, in that we see the gods put to shame by the Name and the

Truth shining forth from the signs—and nothing, insofar as our measure and imagination and organs of perception fall short, and we still see "in a mirror, dimly" and not yet "face to face" (1 Cor 13:12, NKJV).

Blessed be the Lord God, the God of Israel, and blessed be the *revelation of God's glory* forever and ever, and let all the earth be filled with his glory. Amen and Amen (Ps 72:18, 19b).

NOTES

1. The phrase "narrative philosophy" refers to the second part of Franz Rosenzweig's *The Star of Redemption*. The term itself derives from F.W.J. von Schelling (1775–1854).

2. Miskotte has adjusted the translation or made his own.

3. Miskotte quotes here from Ps 105:5 as it appears in the Dutch *Psalmen en Gezangen* (1938).

4. Miskotte here adapts a hymn by Isaac Da Costa (poet, writer, and Jewish convert to Christianity, 1798–1860); it is hymn no. 292 in *Liedboek voor de Kerken* (1973). The translation is ours.

Chapter 12

The Life of Community

1.

We have reached the end of this course. Now must the practice of sharing life together commence within small groups: serious, open, familial, so that kernels of *empowerment* may arise. Both before that happens and then also afterward and continually, a more persistent, regular, and intensive engagement with Scripture will be necessary, an engagement that respects Scripture's self-presentation into multiple "books." It is also possible to approach Scripture as a whole that is yet refracted through *different viewpoints*, all of which are true and pure: as story, as prophecy, as liturgy, as commandment, as epiphany and vision of the world. There is no story that does not include prophecy, there is no prophecy that does not issue in commandment, there is no prophecy that is inconsequential for liturgy and the service of prayer. To discuss each of these would mean a new book, and in any case it will be the theme for our *next* course, namely, how to edify one another, building each other up and galvanizing a better resistance.

There are other options, for example, the beloved practice of English church literature, of imagining the distinctive features of biblical characters.[1] This should not be rejected with a derisive word about "the cult of personality" and "the nineteenth century"! There is also reading Scripture according to the *analogia fidei* or analogy of faith, which may be the most straightforward and fruitful entrée. On this approach, we interpret Scripture with the dogmas of the church and receive guidance from the church's *confession*, so that, for example, we read the gospels according to the teaching of Christ's threefold office of prophet, priest, and king; and we read the apostolic letters according to the order of salvation, justification, sanctification, and glorification; and we read the entirety of Scripture according to the teaching of the Holy Trinity.

These are all possibilities to be recognized, and they will yield fruit, so long as one gives no quarter, not even for an instant, to the *false opposition between teaching and life*. If we learn, we begin to live, consciously; and if we truly live, we live under the inspiration of the teaching. Various ways of accessing and engaging with truth have been practiced in the church and have been tested in practice, such that when one or another does not offer anything fruitful for daily life, it automatically recedes to the background. Every reading method has its appointed time, and even the classic standards like the threefold office need at times to be retired, not to make room for "better" reading methods, but for different ones, which for the community in a certain time period offer a more accessible key to the sanctuary of Scripture. It is our belief that for our particular time, the ABCs, as a spiritual grammar, must take precedence. After that, the other, more dogmatic concepts may be adapted and applied.

2.

I say: dogmatic concepts *follow* from what we have tried to do here, although I also know that they have been practiced long before us and continue regularly during our time, in homilies, meditations, Bible reading, and preaching. It might seem like a particular exigency that we have broached the question of the biblical ABCs and left aside more advanced forms of biblical interpretation in congregations. But we could not have done otherwise, even if we might have preferred to, for we discovered not only an unchurched church (a plague!) but also an unbiblical Bible reading, which is so stiff-necked and self-confident that one grabs one's head and asks how it came so far. Perhaps it is because we are all sectarians, not only the Methodists, who seem to be everywhere,[2] but also the various factions and the Protestant churches themselves, inasmuch as they have refused to listen to biblical interpretation from Roman Catholics, Greek Orthodox, Anglicans, and others? Might the immaturity of our scriptural knowledge, its skew and one-sidedness, be remedied not by striving after "purity" but rather by opening our own one-sidedness to community with the one-sidedness of others? Would this be the prerogative of the ecumenical movement, seeking as it does to enliven contact and conversation between churches? Should the one Catholic Church, apart from its minimum unity in confession and life—which is, qualitatively, a maximum!—also contain a wealth of different "one-sidedness-es," which would cancel or complement one another? Such an expectation would probably obtain, if the attitude of other church families depended on their specific reading of Scripture.

But we should honor particularity! It is precisely in this way of humility and frontier crossing that we arrive at the basic specifications by which to move from *our* Bible to *the* Bible, and so to the unity of Teaching. In general, we, the Dutch, have *far too many opinions*; we "find" this or that, but that which we "find" we have not found by ourselves, nor have we usually found it in Scripture. To a lesser degree, but still clearly noticeable, what Newman once said about his people can be applied to our people:

> the Englishman has opinions. They come from everywhere, some from the children's room, others from the school, others from the world, and he clings to them with zeal because they are his. At least other people make judgments about their opinions, they prove them by referring to some rule: he doesn't care about that at all; he takes them as he finds them . . . but what he absolutely does not want is for someone to *correct* him.[3]

See, that is a bad thing, especially in these changing times. This attitude avenges itself in personal life, it avenges itself above all in the labor of church planting and church leadership. Because not only individuals, but especially congregations must be willing to receive *Weisung*—instruction.

3.

We have a *church*, and we have *individual believers*, but we don't have communities. That is truly a tragic and far-reaching misfortune! We search in vain for little more than very minor traces of living together, of a spiritual community that knows itself and as such stands and acts in the world. Oh, many have already seen it, suffered it, striven against it, and struggled to improve upon it. One person says, we lack community because we lack *charismata*, gifts such as healing and so on, and they tend toward Pentecostalism and similar streams. Another person says—and this is more convincing—what we are missing is participatory *worship*, in which the whole congregation is actively involved. Or: we are missing a stylistic unity, so that ministers are wild and vague, or they are arbitrary and tyrannical in their liturgical leadership. Especially with so introverted a people as the Dutch, the congregation lacks simple courage to join in worship with voice and gesture; by their subdued and personal enjoyment of the spiritual nourishment on offer, the people thus remain monads without windows. Yet another person emphasizes, and with unquestionable right, the need for *reorganization*, in view of the nonsensical notion that the church as a church does not confess what it is supposed to confess by virtue of its name and origin, and that because of the institutional form given to it by the secular government, it cannot attain to new confessions and acts of leadership.[4] And finally, there are many who rightly ascribe the community's ineffectiveness and lack of emancipation to shrunken vision, obliviousness to the needs of the world, and inertia to act as the Acts of the Apostles describes. This diagnosis often coincides with a dogged determination to clear up these problems, considered as personal failings; dogmatic questions are pushed to the background and treated as detrimental to the life of the church, and earnest engagement with them is sometimes even labeled as idolatrous.

Let us heed such voices as the echo of an undeniable emergency, and let us not be too quick to side with one voice against another. Above all let us avoid sharpening our anti-criticism too pointedly, even if it is true that all sides, liturgists as well as activists, are prone to exaggeration.

Sharper distinctions are desirable, and yet, since they would bring us back into "dogmatic" waters, people often advert to missionary matters: they call communities—the same ones they otherwise found unworthy and unsuitable—to give themselves, in one way or another, to *mission*, both internal and external mission, because the world is in extremis and perishing in its need, and yet it remains doggedly silent. So as not to admit its exigency, the world declares and sings that life is but a game.

4.

We can gratefully welcome all these criticisms and these plans for improvement, this critique, concern, and action, as a sure sign of life—as a new dawn and a resurrection from the dead—provided that we also acknowledge the distress of *churchgoers* and agree that "judgment begins with the household of God" (1 Pet 4:17). Judgment in a biblical sense indicates adjudication and discernment and direction. It accomplishes a returning to one's own knowledge, to the original sanctuary. The spiritual gifts, yes, they belong to the church, albeit in other forms than in the first congregation; the liturgical life, yes, we need it to learn how to encounter God again as a sacramental reality. Reorganization, yes! and, of course, action and mission. And yet: we have possibly experienced the new paganism more deeply than others, and we have found it strongly entangled with our human condition and also at the same time furiously hostile to God. Perhaps on account of this, we are shocked in a different way at the condition of church communities.

Here is where *the* front is, running unseen and unacknowledged through our own ranks. The enemy works in secret and entrenches itself in various places and with various outcomes, falling back and waiting for a new opportunity, sometimes in a new and pious armor to "lead astray, if possible, even the elect" (Matt 24:24), let alone the multitude that does not know the Teaching! The multitude is not "cursed," as the Pharisees said (John 7:49), but on the contrary, it provokes God's mercy. Still, the multitude is not equipped to make the right confession or fortified to pursue the good works that belong to such confession. These considerations move us.

The question is: What is the *root*?

The people who take initiative for action and mission, who fill the pews of our churches—are they *convinced* that they, through grace, participate in untraceable and indubitable truth? Do they know anything else in their life that speaks more to them than this incomparable self-disclosure of God? Do they come at times in their own life to true and sacredly foolish acts of goodness, arising out of pure gratitude and childlike wonder at the life that is bestowed upon them? Do they love Jesus? Do they know the radiance, the passion, the earnestness of betrothal? Or—since these may be "exaggerated" expectations again—are they deeply depressed, because they understand so little of it, and secretly think that the world might almost be right? Do they know what they confess? Do they *know* for what truth and what value the church (and they?) might soon have to suffer? Do the faithful churchgoers and participants and interested bystanders and sympathizers *understand* what they hear from the pulpit and what they read in their Bible? (insofar as they still read it! because if the secrets of a thousand homes and inner chambers were revealed, it would be shocking). Can they now, today, give account?

And church leaders? This is said to everyone ordained to the presbyterate: "tend my sheep" (John 21:16). Are they willing? Are they prepared? Are they even concerned about what the time has cast up onto the shore of our experience? Are they embarrassed? Do they ask for more light?

What do the factions in the church—so long as they are indeed mere variations of the confession by which the church stands or falls—mean in the unleashed storm, in the coming chaos, which will not be passive, but active chaos? Is not the *minimum* of faith and knowledge already equivalent to what was seen as the maximum in other, more settled times? *The pious world of so-called church life must come to an end*; what might have been interesting ten years ago—at least as a subject after the break in this or that faction's youth group—has now become provincial, when measured by the elemental violence of spiritual battle.

But perhaps there are no more dangerous people than those who go along with a burning heart and then walk from their place to a wider field and a freer view. For the argument made here does not mean that we discard the Teaching, but rather that we move closer to it. Does the world attack our charity or our work of church praxis? No! The enemy proclaims a teaching, with papal, so to speak, with total and divine authority! And we are stuck with relativism—or else with a misunderstood, "infallible" teaching!

4a.

At first glance one might not think that a book like this one, with its dry and merely formal approach to Scripture, is born out of *terror* and *passion*. But this is the case, and we feel little need to underline its inevitability. What else must take place so that we would open wide our eyes and see what is actually happening—how powerful the onslaught of the storm is and how weak the churches are?

The church, insofar as it is visible and responsible for communicating the gospel, consists today almost exclusively of "clergy": it is, in general, a church of pastors.

But even among the shepherds and teachers themselves, the Teaching can be so darkened that their eyes no longer discern the biblical ABCs clearly. Of the millions of baptized Christians from all nations, only a vanishingly small part remains a part of the Church of God with full earnestness and conviction. Churchgoers represent, again, a small share of those who are more or less consciously joyful that there still exists something like a church. Many from within that wider swathe build their own theology or private religion out of *mutilated remnants from the confession* (plus fragments of sectarian earnestness or liberal ideas, mixed with other wisdoms, as, for example, gained by attending a lecture about China, or through interaction with an Indian friend). In all countries there are remnants of Christian culture that relate to belief. But since they are only vestigial, holdovers from an interior catastrophe, they lack power and fall quickly when a truly fanatical pagan religion throws itself upon them.

So, as long as it is possible, two things must be done:

a proclaim the gospel with strong, broad strokes to the fallen and feral peoples, and pursue mission along several fronts, including a mission that proclaims the truthfulness of God's wrath;
b form, protect, and strengthen core groups of people in the community who are called to the lay apostolate.

5.

Discovering the frailty of these core groups, *in particular at this time*, inspires us to look for resources to help, and we mean human resources, before it is too late. The upright, both near and far, see the *embarrassment* of the church; they see that, even as intellectuals begin to return little by little, the vast majority of the working class remains unmoved, and the farmers fall back in part to their inborn nature-religion.

All of that is bad, especially because, in a disenchanted world, everything has its reason and lies open to understanding. But we do not take it as the worst eventuality; for the confessing church knows what it is—what it has, what its responsibility is, and above all what it intends to do. What it intends is that a core group would grow and *assume* its place in the dreadful contest, and, well-equipped, holding the line, with good reconnaissance, it would *stand fast*. Renewal must come from Scripture, and not through rediscovery of some neglected aspect, not through sophisticated exegesis and spiritual exercise, but through discovering the unity of Scripture in its overall witness. The core groups must wake up, rubbing their eyes and tearing themselves loose from the suggestion of paganism, of natural religion, which rushes all too often through our bloodstream.

For such groups is said what is written at the beginning of Psalm 78 (NRSV, adapt.):

> Give ear, O my people, to my teaching;
>   incline your ears to the words of my mouth.
> I will open my mouth in a *parable*;
>   I will utter dark sayings from of old,
> things that we have heard and *known*,
>   that our *ancestors* have told us.
> We will not hide them from *their* children;
>   we will tell to the coming generation
> the glorious deeds of the Lord, and his might,
>   and the wonders that he has done.
> He established a witness in Jacob,
>   and appointed a Teaching in Israel,
> which he commanded our ancestors
>   to teach to their children;
> that the next generation might *know* them,
>   the children yet unborn,
> (. . .)
> so that they should set their hope in God,
> and not forget the works of God,
>   but keep his commandments;
> and that they should not be like their ancestors,
>   a stubborn and rebellious generation,
> a generation whose heart was not steadfast,
>   whose spirit was not faithful to God.

The psalm does not, plainly, have to do with dogma. It is not about Catholic or Reformed doctrine, but rather about a *sanctified* people's *knowledge*; about the Torah, about the divine virtues, the acts and the commandments of God. Which God? This God who is the God of Israel, who sanctified a new people from out of the nations. We do not require a fence around Torah, but we do now see that for us as for Israel in their diaspora, a *beit midrash* or house of learning is necessary. This house of learning will acquire and preserve, illumine and engage what Holy Scripture tells and depicts—not argues or describes!—about the one and only, the living God, in God's acts and God's real presence in our contemporary world.

Is the lasting, apostolic zeal of an individual conceivable without a community, or at least a core group that is living "under the Word"? Without lay apostles who have a task like that of the company of prophets in ancient Israel? When Luther made the family "evangelical" and put the vicarage in the midst of the congregation, he also performed a social mission, since the *Hauswirtschaft* or home economy still prevailed up until that time. Masters and journeymen, farmers and workers lived in house and garden under one, living Teaching. And now that economic life has slipped away from that chaperone and has assumed complete autonomy, should we content ourselves with specialized youth workers, projects of internal mission, and so on? Nothing can help us but a church made up of living communities, and, through these, home and garden, field and factory and office will be included in mission. Such communities cannot come to life, however, when the *beit midrash*, the house of learning, is missing.

6.

In his encyclical *Acerbo Nimis* (April 15, 1905), Pope Pius X wanted to draw his believers' attention to the urgency of instruction in Christian teaching. He writes as follows:

> Those who still are zealous for the glory of God are seeking the causes and reasons for this decline in religion. Coming to a different explanation, each points out, according to his own view, a different plan for the protection and restoration of the kingdom of God on earth. But while we should not overlook other considerations, We are forced to agree with those who hold that the chief cause of the present *indifference* and, as it were, infirmity of soul, and the serious evils that result from it, is to be found above all in ignorance of things divine. This is fully in accord with what God Himself declared through the Prophet [Hosea]: "And there is no knowledge of God in the land. Thereafter shall the land mourn, and everyone that dwelleth in it shall languish" (Hos 4:1, 3).

And a bit further on, writing about the apostle Paul's warning against the corruption of morals:

> He [Paul] also places the foundation of holiness and sound morals upon a knowledge of divine things—which holds in check evil desires: "See to it therefore,

brethren, that you walk with care: not as unwise but as wise. . . . Therefore, do not become foolish, but understand what the will of the Lord is" (Eph 5:15, 17).

And still further along:

> *Christian teaching* reveals God and His infinite perfection with far greater clarity than is possible by the powers of nature alone . . . Hence the Apostle Paul said: "Christ did not send me to baptize, but to preach the gospel (1 Cor 1:17)," thereby indicating that the first duty of all those who are entrusted in any way with the government of the Church is to instruct the faithful in the things of God.
>
> Here then it is well to emphasize and insist that for a priest there is *no duty more grave or obligation more binding than this*. "For the lips of the priest shall keep knowledge" (Mal 2:7a). The church demands this knowledge of those who are to be ordained to the priesthood. Why? Because the Christian people expect from them knowledge of the divine word, and it was for that end that they were sent by God. "And they shall seek the law at his mouth; because he is the angel of the Lord of Hosts" (Mal 2:7b). Thus the bishop speaking to the candidates for the priesthood in the ordination ceremony says: Let your teaching be a spiritual remedy for God's people; and thus meditating day and night on His law, they may believe what they read, and teach what they shall believe.
>
> We are indeed aware that the work of teaching the Catechism is unpopular with many because as a rule it is deemed of little account and for the reason that it does not lend itself easily to the winning of public praise. But this in Our opinion is a judgment based on vanity and devoid of truth. We do not disapprove of those pulpit orators who, out of genuine zeal for the glory of God, devote themselves to defense of the faith and to its spread . . . But their labor presupposes labor of another kind, that of the catechist. And so if this be lacking, then the foundation is wanting; *and they labor in vain who build the house* (Ps 127:1).
>
> It is much easier to find a preacher capable of delivering an eloquent and elaborate discourse than a catechist who can impart a catechetical instruction which is praiseworthy in every detail . . . They are mistaken who think that because of inexperience and lack of training of the people the work of catechizing can be performed in a slipshod fashion. On the contrary, the less educated the hearers, the more zeal and diligence must be used to adapt the sublime truths to their untrained minds; these truths, indeed, far surpass the natural understanding of the people, yet must be known by all—the uneducated and the cultured—in order that they may arrive at eternal happiness.
>
> It will not do to say, in excuse, that faith is a free gift of God bestowed upon each one . . . Man has the faculty of understanding at his birth, but he also has need of *his mother's word* to awaken it, as it were, and to make it active. So too, the Christian, born again of water and the Holy Spirit, has faith within him, but he requires the word of the teaching church to nourish and develop it and to make it bear fruit.[5]

7.

We have given this bundle of quotations, because they express great pastoral care—and because they place a finger on the wound. Certainly we as Protestants (i.e., those who testify [*test*] in favor [*pro*] of the unabridged and unmixed gospel) are already in a more advanced stage of trouble. On the other hand, such vast ignorance as, we may perhaps say, exists among the masses in Roman lands is not found with us. We cannot, as this encyclical does, speak about "things" and "truths" as the object of faith, since this is contrary not only to a few biblical texts but to the entire structure of Scripture. We cannot, as this letter does, align the Word so closely with the "law." We also see the "decay of morals" welling up from even deeper sources; and of course further differences could be mentioned.

Still, this encyclical expresses *a concern for catechesis* and a corresponding pastoral interest in *empowering* the congregation, which characterized the Reformed churches from their outset. We notice a parting of ways between the Roman and Reformed approaches to pastoral care, if we compare these beautiful quotes to the thought we developed in the first chapter, which is more important than ever: that the church is not only subject but also the recipient of the teaching, and that the church must engage not only in *lehren*, teaching, but also in *lernen*, learning.

Thank God it is not true and it cannot be true that the church or the hierarchy or the highest bishop must continually seek and find or receive that which serves as eternal blessing and peace for the church itself and also for the nations. God has not left the church in such loneliness with itself and with its treasures. The holy Teaching is a guide, a world to dwell in, both for us personally and for the community.

A more striking difference with our *present* situation comes to the fore when we consider that the encyclical quoted above does *not* reckon with the "science" of the new pagan religion; so, too, the encyclical regards the Teaching as the teaching of the church, its doctrine, and not Scripture in its independent self-testimony, let alone in its elementary power and its *grondvormen* or ground-forms. This observation is not meant as a partisan reproach. In spite of good work that has been carried out in recent years, the teaching documents and catechetical materials of our church contain hardly a trace awareness that Scripture is *wholly anti-pagan testimony*, repelling the natural religion of the human heart.

8.

These two things are closely related: the awakening of the instinctive power of paganism in human hearts—and the retreat of the church to the elementary character of the scriptural *oerwoorden* or primary words. Anyone who sees and understands this relationship will not be surprised to hear that we consider ecumenical initiatives and liturgical reforms and church reorganizing, and even the commission to mission, to be of secondary importance in comparison with this single goal: that we learn again to "live under the Word": learning, not privately but together, in the *beit midrash* or house of learning, to spell the ABCs. This is the experience of the Confessing Church in Germany: the very life of the congregation depends on such knowledge and praxis: to learn, maybe starting again from the very beginning, as Israel once had to do, where the *Name* intervenes, where exactly the break from the natural religion of the pagan, carnal, human heart takes place.

The "sanctification of the Name" is the commandment of our time, as it is in all ages, but now all of life is led back to it. Confession once again becomes a fundamental act. Anyone who wishes more precisely to envision the life of community on the front lines, defending the trenches, must read the important book by Oskar Hammelsbeck. A remarkable lay preacher, he wrote *der Kirchliche Unterricht*, "The Church Teaching," in 1939.[6] For seven years he also led a major institute for general education, then worked in the unemployment office [*Erwerblosen-kameradschaften*] and in camps of the Voluntary Labor Service [*Freiwilligen Arbeitsdienstes*], a public works program. From questions of cultural and social nature he was driven on to *Seelsorge*, the cure of souls. As part of that pastoral practice, he considered how modern people in house and school and trade unions can be brought to a life "under the Word." Only in this way can the convulsion, the *overestimation of principles and parties* be overcome; only in this way is *Frömmelei* or pietism pushed aside and space created for what Hammelsbeck calls *echte Weltlichkeit*, true worldliness. Scripture bespeaks a sobriety and practicality. The Teaching instructs the community in worldly living, which means: living in the world in such a way that one does not aggrandize it into a demonic, divine power, but rather, considers nothing as objectionable in itself, provided it is received with thanksgiving (1 Tim 4:4). Sanctified life consists in such as this.

The issue at stake is clear: the *life* of the church. Not the existence of the church per se, but the life of the community. Not the mystical life or praxis, considered on their own, but the unity of both through the activity and guidance of Word and Spirit. "Living under the Word" is different from speaking about the Word. It is *living* in a particular way, living as *community* in freedom and bondedness that proceed from the accompanying Presence and from the Word that calls, guides, heals, and creates. That is why *Bible study groups* can play a role in *spiritually activating* congregations. That was also the rationale for this course. Even though the material we discussed might initially have seemed dry, it concerned the essential matters of faith and was full already of spiritual decision. As soon as we understand Scripture as holy Teaching, we are faced with these decisions; as soon as we experience the structure of Scripture by scrutinizing it word for word, it becomes a rampart against our own, innate paganism; as soon as we recognize the whole goal of Scripture, which makes one interlinking, frontal attack against our wrongful living-and-thinking: the same bondage from out of which God once led Israel, and into which we are now, after so many centuries of apparent peace, threatening to fall back.

9.

We already mentioned this harsh sentence: there is a church and there are believers, but there are few, if any, *communities*. One may contest the point. We hope that the contesters are right, but we do not agree with them in advance if they present the usual arguments, for example, the Word is administered, so the church is there. Yes, there is preaching, but there is no empowerment, and the hearers are defenseless against all kinds of strange teachings (Eph 4:14). Or, it could be the case that there is empowerment, but it is the empowerment of those who assertively defend various factions in the church, which results in stultifying doctrine or flying into eerie, perfunctory action.

We seem to be stuck in a *vicious cycle* of supply and demand. We don't know what, biblically speaking, counts as teaching, and consequently we don't want teaching; and we never find out what teaching actually is. We have a particular taste, and that taste is so banal that our pastor has to adapt, and so the pastor does, so that preaching itself becomes banal. Or: to "modern" people, the entirety of Scripture sounds too wild, and they no longer listen to it; a modern preacher therefore adapts, and, compensatorily, gets more and more ingenious, and so strays further off course. We don't have a liturgical order, it is alien to us, and hence we don't long to have one; as such, everything that is "new" becomes an annoyance, and we fail to implement it on account of "those who are weak." Likewise, we don't have a well-planned catechetical practice, and everyone does what is right in their own eyes. So one might also say: we have no communities, no solidarity in the Spirit, no shared life "under the Word."

9a.

If we reckon only with what we discern directly, the empirical church could drive us to despair, not least through the law of inertia, according to which the unbiblical Bible reading continues. But our complaint in itself bears witness to a different church, the invisible one, which lives hidden *within* the visible, all-too-visible. Our complaints witness to a divine *sanctification* that takes place in the midst of the human—the all-too-human.

We do not lack the experience of standing in the middle of the steppe and hearing a voice say, "take off your shoes, because the place on which you stand is holy ground" (Exod 3:5)! Sometimes it doesn't take all that much to experience that the uneven ground shall become level and the rough places, a plain (Isa 40:4). We can expect to encounter the *in*visible nowhere else than in the *visible*; that is why no sensible person thinks first of *planting* new churches—no, they pray in faith that that life will return or be revealed to the old church communities. The valley will replace the high places (cf. Isa 40:4), and the desert will blossom like a rose (Isa 35:1).

A church father once said:

> The road which leads from the outward form of the church to its mystery, from her two-sided visible and public character to her true nature, unity, and holiness, is the road of faith. This road cannot be avoided . . . If we do not take it, we are doomed here as elsewhere to sway about hopelessly, as on a see-saw, between the extremities of a foolish optimism and a foolish pessimism. In that case we are members of the church, today eager and enthusiastic and tomorrow tired and sceptical. *Members*? No, not members, but *spectators*, keen today and tired tomorrow, comparable with the spectators of a game, at one moment clapping and at another booing, interested perhaps owing to some bet on the result, but with it all merely showing that they are not really taking part in the game, but merely looking on. The players themselves have not taken on bets, are not clapping or booing but are playing. That is what taking part means, and it is just the same in the church to take part in the life of the church means to have faith. Our faith is what decides that we are members of the church and not mere spectators. And it is precisely faith which decides that we are taking a part not only in the visible, public form of the church, but at the same time in its true nature, unity and holiness. By assenting in faith to Jesus Christ as our Lord, we have already received and given ourselves the answer to the question about the one, true and holy church. We have then sought and found the church in Him as her Head, far beyond all visible human greatness or all visible human misery.[7]

The church *is* the church by faith in *becoming* the church, again and again. We do not want to be spectators, we desire that communities transform from spectators into participants. Into *life*! Through the *Word*! As Hammelsback has said: "Muzzled words will not do, but rather the word lived out by sanctification."[8]

"Sleeper, awake! Rise from the dead, and Christ will shine on you" (Eph 5:14). This is what it comes down to; this is the purpose of the holy Teaching that offers itself to us again, the purpose of the spontaneously forming core groups. If they are guided by faithful and patient leaders, we believe that we have much good to await from them, though their beginning is very humble.

The Teaching is in the midst! A breakthrough of habit and a danger to lonely reading! The Teaching, the holy Teaching, as companion and guide!

Practically speaking, the enemy now assaulting us does not target dogma. He focuses his artillery on a much easier target: on the Israelite profile of Scripture, on the unity of the testaments. He is aggravated by this God, who is not the All; he is aggravated by these Virtues, all of it gets on his nerves. Therefore our spiritual defense must also be much more elementary; we must learn that the anti-pagan character of Scripture and the impossibility of natural theology are *all-decisive*. The terrible tradeoff between coercion and freedom, between prostration before Nature and the expectation of Glory, still continues. But those living "under the Word" have already made the simple and clear decision.

Hence the turn to the biblical ABCs. We will say it once more—we do not turn to the ABCs because no further training in the church's doctrine is necessary; a new "catechism" of sorts will have to be written for adults, comparable to the catechism of Trent and as comprehensive as Sertillanges's *Catéchisme des Incroyants* [The Unbelievers' Catechism].[9] Courses about all questions pertaining to the life of church and nation remain desirable, as does a compact reading of all of Holy Scripture, which we will attempt later on. Still: we are persuaded that as a tool, the biblical ABCs must take tactical and factual precedence. On what grounds? Because the road to the epic battle of spirits starts there, and it is the shortest and *best-protected*. It leads from an anguished defense to a spirited *offensive*.

In this course we did not yet speak about the Teaching itself (Chapter 2 only concerns the word: Teaching); for that, we would need carefully to read each part of Scripture with each other part. Every story bears within it the living content of the Teaching. Our reading and living together would attest that reality. And yet already in this preparatory grammar you may have sensed the breath of God's love, the God who, in the Teaching, accompanies us in all of our life. From afar, perhaps, you heard the murmur of the Teaching as the source of life, of living discipline, of living virtue, and living action. Instruction is letting oneself be aligned under the healing power of the One who alone knows what is right, who alone has the right to direct, and who alone directs our life.

10.

The *life* of the community was from the beginning a life of love lived by "continuing steadfastly in the apostles' teaching" (Acts 2:42): by pressing into the *viva vox* of their testimony, which is sealed and finalized and confirmed by the Spirit. God is, as God shows *through* loving acts, the One who loves, *rising up early* (Jer 7:13; 11:7; 32:22) to teach us. *Here* is where it happens, where the miracle of *love* seizes hold of us—this love that is knowledge, and this knowledge that is love. Such knowledge comes from this: that we *are* known. If only we possessed this love! We would find in ourselves a great awakening. And in this *awakening* of our spirit, we would taste the awakening of the world and of all things. After all, we do not awake for ourselves alone—none of us lives to ourselves, and we do not die to ourselves (Rom 14:7). The love of God that wakes up under the Word and that is kept awake through the Word, also *awakens* what is dead in us and outside of us, and raises it to new life. Whoever knows love once, seeks and finds its trail everywhere, meets its sorrows and joys everywhere; for that person, everything is meaningful and fascinating, full of essence, power, help, and reference to the horizon. This is the sign that love is real: that it lives in the Presence of the One who loves, and in this Presence, all of life receives a *face*, and the acts of God become, in our eyes, eternal signs that will not be destroyed.

The singularity, the unity, the concord will grow and break forth—from the Teaching.

Once, there was a time when we spoke half-ironically about "Bible-believing" people, and then a period arrived in which those people seem indispensable to us. In the past, we used to talk of "old wives' tales" (1 Tim 4:7) that were at odds with good teaching. But now we realize that there are also ancient human, antique-heroic tales, which not only disrupt sound teaching but also simple human life. We used to fear separation from the world so much that we hardly allowed ourselves time to reflect; the order of the day now is, reflection! Especially if one takes to heart that the world is running amok. Finally and at last: it is not the case that many religions exist, and that one of them is so-called Christendom. There is—and we must know this by heart—a natural religion in many forms, and there is, by grace, faith in the Name.

One man's meat is another man's poison. Christ must increase and we must decrease.

The more firmly we believe in the Name, the more unbelieving we become toward the primordial powers of life. That is why we want to learn. The more still that we become before God's acts, the more activity will go out from us also. This is why we seek the companionship and guidance of the Teaching. The less we have of our own knowledge, the closer we can come to one another. This is the reason why those who are very alienated from each other discover one other again in these times. Whoever has faithfully attended the *beit midrash* or house of learning will become a great warrior, and will perform great deeds. And whoever carries the Song of Songs within them will go out and bind up the battered human face wherever it may be found. We turn at the very end once more to the litany on the Torah, the holy Teaching (Ps 119, NRSV adapt.):

Blessed are those whose way is blameless,
> who walk in the law of the Lord.
Blessed are those who keep his decrees,
> who seek him with their whole heart,
I delight in the way of your decrees
> as much as in all riches.
Deal bountifully with your servant,
> so that I may live and observe your word.
I live as an alien in the land;
> do not hide your commandments from me.
I shall walk at liberty,
> for I have sought your precepts.
I will also speak of your decrees before kings,
> and shall not be put to shame;
Hot indignation seizes me because of the wicked,
> those who forsake your law.
Your statutes have been my songs
> in the house of my pilgrimage.
I remember your name in the night, O Lord,
> and keep your law.
The arrogant smear me with lies,
> revive me according to your word.
It is good for me that I was humbled,
> so that I might learn your statutes.
The unfolding of your words gives light;
> it imparts understanding to the simple.
With open mouth I pant,
> because I long for your commandments.
I have seen a limit to all perfection,
> but your commandment is exceedingly broad.

NOTES

1. Miskotte refers to the genre of "Scripture Biography" (or: "Bible Biography"), which flourished in nineteenth-century Britain and America.

2. Miskotte refers to various holiness movements that originated from North American Methodism. These movements exercised considerable influence (and ignited controversy) in the Dutch Reformed Church while Miskotte worked in Amsterdam. Contrary to his wording here, Miskotte looked quite favourably on these movements.

3. John Henry Newman, *Sermons Preached on Various Occasions* (London: Burns and Lambert, 1858), 174.

4. The church order for the *Hervormde Kerk* was issued in 1816 by the king, Willem I. Long-felt dissatisfaction with this church order led eventually to the adoption of the new church order in 1951.

5. The English translation of Pius X's encycical *Acerbo nimis* (1905) is taken from the Vatican website: http://www.vatican.va/content/pius-x/en/encyclicals/documents/hf_p-x_enc_15041905_acerbo-nimis.html. Italics are not in the original text but are added by Miskotte.

6. Oskar Hammelsbeck, *Leben unter dem Wort als Frage des Kirchlichen Unterrichts*, Theologische Existenz heute 55 (Munich: Christian Kaiser Verlag, 1938). Hammelsbeck (1899-1975) was the leader of the Confessing Church in Berlin.

7. Karl Barth, *The Knowledge of God and the Service of God According to the Teaching of the Reformation, Recalling the Scottish Confession of 1560: The Gifford Lectures Delivered in the University of Aberdeen in 1937 and* 1938, trans. J.L.M. Haire and Ian Henderson (London: Hodder and Stoughton Publishers, 1938), 158–159. In the Dutch original, Miskotte quotes from the German text and supplies his own translation.

8. Hammelsbeck, *Leben unter dem Wort,* 52.

9. A.D. Sertillanges, *Le Catéchisme des incroyants*, 2 vols. (Paris: Flammarion, 1930). Sertillanges (1863–1948) was a French Dominican who was well-known for his studies on Aquinas.

Appendix
Log of Additions to the 1941 Edition

CHAPTER 1

- Page 1: In the dark winter of 1940 [1941: "in the dark winter"]
- Page 3: What hinders us, that we misunderstand this authority? [1941 lacks this paragraph entirely]
- Page 4: Rather, we ask from after the fact, dependent on the content of Scripture [1941: "authority" instead of "content"]
- Page 5: I want to press this point even further: we are experiencing again how much we are connected with Israel through the holy Instruction that we have received from God [1941 lacks this sentence]
- Page 5: About which we can never marvel enough. Where did it all come from? [1941 lacks this note about Luther, which, in the postwar version connects to a following paragraph about "religion"]

CHAPTER 2

- Page 12: and Scripture is complete in itself and contains instruction concerning our reality and the One with whom we have to do [1941 lacks this clause]
- Page 13: and nor can it now [1941 lacks this phrase]
- Page 13: defenseless in the face of new questions that are hurled against us [1941 lacks the word "defenseless"]
- Page 16: of the ABCs [1941 lacks this phrase]

CHAPTER 3

- Page 18: generically religious [1941 lacks this phrase]

- Page 19: They are there, but they are not yours [1941 lacks the second phrase]
- Page 19: But here the Name encloses the absolute power of salvation [1941 lacks "salvation"]
- Page 19: everlasting will to save [1941 has "everlasting truth"]
- Page 20: True and faithful self-revelation [1941 lacks these descriptors]
- Page 20: At last, finding themselves in an empty, ghostly world, their will to live will ebb [1941 lacks this sentence]
- Page 22: In distinction from that which is "given" [1941 lacks this phrase]

CHAPTER 4

- Page 28: philosophical endeavor [1941 features just "philosophy"]
- Page 28: grounded in God's holy decision [1941 has "Eternal Being"]
- Page 28: the godhead of ancient and modern naturalism [1941 lacks the adjectives]
- Page 29: and moving outwards from that epicenter [1941 lacks this phrase]
- Page 29: We are thus naturally inclined to consider YHWH [1941 has "Jehova en Jezus"]
- Page 30: El Shaddai appears as a negative expression [1941 lacks the description "negative expression"]
- Page 32: or some contingent event [1941 lacks this phrase]
- Page 32: in the depths of divine constancy and faithfulness [1941 has only "eternity"]

CHAPTER 5

- Page 40: the miracle of the holy Teaching [1941 has "intimate miracle"]
- Page 41: There, in *song* [1941 lacks these words]
- Page 42: with a sequence of divine acts for the sake of the earth [1941 lacks the final prepositional phrase]

CHAPTER 6

- Page 46: the unity of divine virtues is in and of itself no virtue [1941 has "divine attributes"]
- Page 48: that the Messiah is called [1941 features only "He"]
- Page 50: God is created or understood [1941 lacks "or understood"]

Appendix 153

CHAPTER 7

- Page 58: such as "biblical infallibility" [1941 lacks this phrase]

CHAPTER 8

- Page 71: also the sobriety of pure logic, which only mathematical logic can topple from its pride of place [1941 lacks the phrase about "pride of place"]
- Page 73: only a perpetual receptivity to the Saving-Word, which has gone out into the world in calling, judging, and healing, will be able to keep our reading, learning, and life in the right path [1941 adds parentheses and parentheses-within-parentheses to this sentence: "Only a perpetual receptivity to the Saving-Word, which has gone into the world in calling, judging, and healing (and which appears eventually in this order and articulation [in a literal way] as the creating word) will be able to keep our reading, learning and life in the right path"]

CHAPTER 9

- Page 80: do not know the way [1941 lacks this phrase]
- Page 83: from the place where YHWH founded a memorial for the divine name (Exod 20:24) [1941 has instead here: "from the revelation of the Messiah, the Christ"]
- Page 83: where God's trace in history has left an impression ... [1941 has a much simpler statement: "Once more—for it is clearer here than anywhere else in the holy Teaching—we understand this Way rightly only from the Middle, this is from the revelation of the Messiah, the Christ. In him the whole fullness of deity dwells bodily (Col 2:8)"]

CHAPTER 10

- Page 88: and it hardly even appreciates humans as partner to God [1941 lacks the mention of "partner to God"]
- Page 91: within the parameters of this book [1941 refers to an evening lecture]
- Page 100: It is an answer to the call [1941 has here "answer to the sanctification"]
- Page 103: It is proclamation: proclamation of the covenant [1941 lacks this sentence]

CHAPTER 11

- Page 115: makes public what was hidden [1941 has only, "the second Coming is decisive"]

Bibliography

Barth, Karl. "The Church and the War: A Letter by Professor Karl Barth to a French Pastor." *Theology* 237 (1940): 209–217.

———. "Eine Frage und eine Bitte an die Protestanten von Frankreich." In *Eine Schweizer Stimme 1938–1945*, 147–156. Zürich: EVZ, 1945.

———. *The Knowledge of God and the Service of God According to the Teaching of the Reformation, Recalling the Scottish Confession of 1560: The Gifford Lectures Delivered in the University of Aberdeen in 1937 and 1938*. Translated by J.L.M. Haire and Ian Henderson. London: Hodder and Stoughton Publishers, 1938.

———. *Lutherfeier 1933*. Theologische Existenz heute 4. München: Chr. Kaiser Verlag, 1933.

———. *Offene Briefe 1935–1942*. Edited by Diether Koch. Karl Barth Gesamtausgabe Abt. V, Briefe. Zürich: TVZ, 2001.

Bavinck, Herman. *Reformed Dogmatics, Vol 2: God and Creation*. Translated by John Vriend. Grand Rapids: Baker Academic, 2004.

Breukelman, Frans. *Debharim: der biblische Wirklichkeitsbegriff des Seins in der Tat*. Biblische Theologie II/1. Kampen: Kok, 1998.

Brod, Max. *Heidentum, Christentum, Judentum: ein Bekenntnisbuch*. 2 Vols. München: Kurt Wolff Verlag, 1921.

Cleveringa, Rudolph P. "Rede naar aanleiding van het ontslag van prof. Mr. E.M. Meijers, uitgesproken op 26 november 1940, als Decaan van de Juridische Faculteit." *Leids Universiteits Blad* 11 (1945): 5–13.

de Vries, Jan. "Boekbeoordelingen: K.H. Miskotte, *Edda en Thora*." *Nieuw Theologisch Tijdschrift* 29 (1940): 151–157.

Drews, Arthur. *Die deutsche Spekulation seit Kant*. 2 Vols. Berlin: P. Maeter, 1893.

Fichte, Johann Gottlieb. "On the Ground of Our Belief in a Divine World-Governance." In *J.G. Fichte and the Atheism Dispute (1798–1800)*, edited by Yolanda Estes and Curtis Bowman, 17–30. London: Ashgate, 2010.

Green, Emma. "A Christian Insurrection." *The Atlantic*, Jan. 8, 2021. www.theatlantic.com/politics/archive/2021/01/evangelicals-catholics-jericho-march-capitol/617591/

Hammelsbeck, Oskar. *Leben unter dem Wort als Frage des Kirchlichen Unterrichts.* Theologische Existenz heute 55. Munich: Christian Kaiser Verlag, 1938.
Hugo, Victor. *The Hunchback of Notre Dame.* Edited by Keith Wren. Wordsworth Classics. Hertfordshire: Wordsworth, 2004.
Kohlbrugge, H.F. *Wozu das Alte Testament? Anleitung zur richtigen Schätsung der Bücher Mosis und der Propheten.* Elberfeld: Verlag der Niederländischen reformierten Gemeinde, 1855.
Koopmans, Jan. "Bijna te laat!" In *Het verzet der Hervormde Kerk*, edited by H.C. Touw, 2:209–216. 2 Vols. Gravenhage: Boekencentrum, 1946.
———. "Boekbespreking K.H. Miskotte, *Bijbelsch ABC.*" *Kerkbeurtenblad voor Amsterdam en omgeving* 16 (1942): 20.
———. *Wat zegt de Bijbel?* Amsterdam, 1941.
Leopold, J.H. "Een lucht van marmer en van onyxsteen." In *Verzen, Fragmenten*, edited by P.N. van Eyck and Johan B.W. Polak, 313. Verzameld Werk, Part 2. Brusse: Rotterdam/Van Oorschot: Amsterdam, 1951–1952.
Miskotte, K.H. *Als de goden zwijgen: Over de zin van het Oude Testament.* Amsterdam: uitgeversmaatschappiij Holland, 1956.
———. "Betere weerstand." In *Het verzet der Hervormde Kerk*, edited by H.C. Touw, 2: 222–227. 2 Vols. Gravenhage: Boekencentrum, 1946.
———. *Biblisches ABC: Wider das unbiblische Bibellesen.* Translated by Hinrich Stoevesandt. Neurkirch-Vluyn: Neukirchener Verlag, 1976.
———. *Edda en Thora: een vergelijking van Germaanse en Israëlitische religie.* Nijkerk: C.F. Callenbach, 1939.
———. *Edda und Thora: ein Vergleich germanischer und israelischer Religion.* Translated by Heinrich Braunschweiger. Berlin: LIT Verlag, 2015.
———. "Die Erlaubnis zum schriftgemäßem Denken." In *Antwort: Festschrift zum 70 Geburtstag von Karl Barth*, edited by Eduard Thurneysen, 29–51. Zürich: EVZ, 1956.
———. "Het jodendom als vraag aan de kerk." *Eltheto* 88 (1933/34): 6.
———. *Karl Barth: Inspiratie en vertolking: Inleidingen, essays, briefwisseling.* Verzameld Werk Vol. 2. Kampen: Kok 1987.
———. *Messiaansch verlangen: Het lyrisch werk van Henriëtte Roland Holst.* Amsterdam: Uitgeverij Holland, 1941.
———. *Messiaans verlangen en andere literatuur en cultuurkritische opstellen.* Verzameld Werk Vol. 12. Kampen: Kok, 1999.
———. "Opmerkingen over theologische exegese." In *De openbaring der verborgenheid*, edited by M.C. Slotemaker de Bruïne, 63–99. Baarn: Bosch & Keuning, 1934.
———. "Das Problem der theologischen Exegese." In *Theologische Aufsätze: Karl Barth zum 50. Geburtstag*, edited by Ernst Wolf, 51–77. München: Chr. Kaiser, 1936.
———. *Theologische opstellen.* Verzameld Werk Vol. 9. Kampen: Kok, 1990.
———. *Uit de dagboeken 1938–1940.* Verzameld Werk Vol. 5c. Utrecht: Kok, 2018.
———. *Wenn die Götter schweigen: vom Sinn des Alten Testaments.* Translated by Heinrich Stoevesandt. München: Chr. Kaiser Verlag, 1966.

———. *Das Wesen der jüdischen Religion*. Translated by Heinrich Braunschweiger. Berlin: LIT Verlag, 2017.
———. *Het Wezen der Joodsche Religie*. Amsterdam: Paris, 1933.
———. *When the Gods are Silent*. Translated by John W. Doberstein. New York: Harper and Row, 1967.
Newman, John Henry. *Sermons Preached on Various Occasions*. London: Burns and Lambert, 1858.
Nietzsche, Friedrich W. *Also sprach Zarathustra*. KSA 4. Berlin: de Gruyter, 1988.
Pius, X. "Acerbo Nimis." *The Holy See*, April 15, 1905. https://www.vatican.va/content/pius-x/en/encyclicals/documents/hf_p-x_enc_15041905_acerbo-nimis.html
Posner, Sarah. "How the Christian Right Helped Foment Insurrection." *Rolling Stone*, Jan. 31, 2021. https://www.rollingstone.com/culture/culture-features/capitol-christian-right-trump-1121236/
Rosenzweig, Franz. *The Star of Redemption*. Translated by William W. Hallo. Notre Dame, IN: Notre Dame University Press, 1970.
Sertillanges, A.D. *Le Catéchisme des incroyants*. 2 Vols. Paris: Flammarion, 1930.
Simon, Mallory and Sarah Sidner. "Decoding the extremist symbols and groups at the Capitol Hill insurrection." *CNN*, Jan. 11, 2011. https://www.cnn.com/2021/01/09/us/capitol-hill-insurrection-extremist-flags-soh/index.html
Spengler, Oswald. *The Decline of the West*. Vol. I. Translated by Charles Francis Atkinson. Alfred A Knopf, 1926.
Spinoza, Baruch. *Ethics*. Translated by W.H. White, revised by A.H. Stirling. Wordsworth Classics of World Literature. Ware: Wordsworth, 2001.
van der Meiden, Willem. "*Bijbels ABC*, een polemische grammatica." *In de Waagschaal* 46 (2017): 1, 7–10.
van Roon, Ger. *Protestants Nederland en Duitsland 1933–1941*. Utrecht/Antwerpen: Het Spectrum, 1973.

Scripture Index

Old Testament
Genesis
1:1, 29, 79
1:3, 67
2–4, 101
2:1–3, 62
2:7, 110
3:9, 68
4:9, 74
4:15, 122
5, 12
5:22, 24, 112
9:12, 122
9:13, 122
9:17, 100, 122
11:4, 74
12:1, 70
17:1, 112
17:5, 18
17:11, 122
17:22, 110
19:17, 124
21:33, 22
28:12, 93
32:24, 93
49:18, 118

Exodus
3:4, 71
3:5, 89, 101, 145
3:12, 105
3:14, 27, 94
3:15b, 28, 29, 114
4:31, 120
13:19, 120
15, 62
15:3, 18, 43
15:11, 92
16:35, 115
19:6, 93, 97
20:1, 68
20:5, 36, 89
20:7, 18, 22
20:11, 93
20:24, 22, 83
23:20, 18
25:15, 80
25:30, 103
29:34, 37, 96
31:3, 18
33:11–15, 82
34:6–7, 40
40:34, 115

Leviticus
16:4, 96
18:21, 18

19:12, 18
20:7, 98
21:7, 96
22:32, 97
24:11, 18
26:12, 41, 112
27, 96
27:21, 93, 96
27:30, 96
27:32, 96

Numbers
5:17, 96
15:30, 97
16:3, 93, 96
16:5, 96
16:22, 3, 100
27:17, 3

Deuteronomy
1:30, 33, 112
8:3, 69
12:11, 23
28:9, 112
28:58, 19
30:11–15, 2
32:4, 43, 61
32:10, 102
32:11, 43
32:39, 71

Joshua
3:11, 13, 105
20:7, 97
23:14, 83
24:17, 122

Judges
6:34, 31

Ruth
1:6, 120
1:20, 18

1 Samuel
2:6, 71
2:11, 105
2:21, 120
3:4, 71
4:7, 119
10:7, 122
21:6, 93, 96
23:10, 42

2 Samuel
22:31a, 79

1 Kings
2:2, 83
8:33, 19
8:39, 42
9:4, 112

2 Kings
13:19, 42

1 Chronicles
16:10, 18
16:33, 119
29:14b, 102

2 Chronicles
20:9, 18
30:17, 97
33:4, 18

Ezra
9:6, 121

Job
general reference, 30
19:25, 23

Psalms
1:2, 12
1:6, 42
2:1–2, 55

2:3, 74
2:6, 115
2:7, 31
2:11, 105
2:12, 31
3:5, 92
5:11, 128
5:12, 19
7:9, 42
8:1, 22
8:5, 120
9:18, 118
17:8, 82
19:8–10a, 11
20:5, 128
20:7, 92
22:4, 5, 92
22:6, 121
23:1, 43
24:1, 105, 106
25:3, 117, 121
25:4, 84
25:5, 117
25:7, 21
25:8b, 9, 13–14
25:9, 84
25:21, 117
27:14, 118
28:2, 92
32:8, 7
33:6, 69
33:9, 71
34:4, 19
40:15, 121
46:8, 61
48:3, 115
49:12, 110
50:2, 119
50:3, 119
56:10, 69
50:1, 20
50:3, 66
52, 42

52:11, 19
65:9, 106
65:10, 120
65:14, 128
67:5, 128
68:16, 102
69:7, 121
70:3, 121
72:10–12, 61
72:15, 124
72:17, 113
72:18, 132
72:19, 23, 105, 132
73, 121
74:19, 82
77:13a, 79
78, 139
78:11, 61
78:43, 122
78:65, 43
81:14, 42, 112
82, 8
82:1, 20
83:17, 19
84:12, 43
85:10–11, 113
86:11, 84
86:14–15, 41
86:8, 20
86:11, 18, 22
87:5, 115
89:5, 97
89:12, 105
89:19, 92
89:51, 65, 83
92, 60
93–99, 127
95:1, 128
95:3, 20
95:10, 84
96:13, 119
98:9, 119
100:1, 128

100:2, 105
100:3, 25, 30
101:6, 112
102:26, 110
103:7, 41, 61
103:12, 31
104:24, 107
104:31, 107
104:35, 106
105, 52
105:3, 18, 92
105:5, 132
106, 52
106:4, 120
107, 52
110:3, 115
111:7, 61
111:9, 92
118:17–20, 62
119, 7, 147–48
119:11, 7
119:14, 84
119:37b, 79
119:43, 7
119:96, 10
119:105, 7
121:1, 119
122, 115
122:4, 19
127:1, 141
130:4, 96
132:13, 102
136:1, 72
136:2, 20
138:1, 20
138:5a, 80
145:1, 2, 21, 44
145:8, 41
147:16, 14
147:18–20, 14
150, 127

Proverbs
6:22, 112
8:22, 79
8:35, 9, 124
8:36b, 9
14:16, 112
18:10, 22
23:26, 10

Ecclesiastes
1:4, 105
3:19, 111
12:5, 111
12:12, 6

Song of Songs
general reference, 51, 52, 55n2, 147
8:6–7, 52

Isaiah
2:1, 113
6:3, 92, 105
6:5, 71
7:14, 122
8:13, 90
9:5, 113
9:6, 48
9:8, 68
11:1–9, 113
11:4b, 69
21:11, 120
23:18, 97
24:23, 121
25:6, 113
26:8, 19, 22, 79
26:11, 121
26:13, 22
29:23, 95
31:3, 100
31:4, 43
32:15–17, 113
33:22, 43
35:1, 145
35:2, 128
35:6, 128
38:7, 122
38:19, 124
40:3, 79

40:4, 145
40:6b, 69
40:8a, 69
40:30–31, 118
41:4, 126
41:14, 95
43:1, 68, 71
43:3, 95
43:11, 71
44:6, 126
44:23, 128
45:1, 31
47:4, 18, 95
48:12, 126
48:17, 95
49:7, 95
49:13, 128
50:7, 121
54:5, 43, 95
55:8b–9, 79
57:11, 66
61:10, 43
62:1, 66
63:16, 31
64:8, 31
65:6, 66

Jeremiah
1:6, 71
2:13, 43
3:23, 130
6:4, 97, 98
7:13, 147
11:7, 147
14:8–9, 118
17:5, 100
17:10, 42
20:11, 121
22:7, 97
22:29, 71
29:11, 118
31:3, 95
32:17, 33
32:22, 147
51:48, 128

Lamentations
3:25, 118

Ezekiel
16:4–15, 53
20:12, 97
37:28, 97

Daniel
7:18, 97

Hosea
1:10, 71
4:1–3, 140
4:6, 71
11:1, 71
11:9, 92

Joel
2:28, 116

Amos
5:6, 8, 107
8:11–12, 69

Micah
4:1–5, 112–13

Nahum
1:3b–5, 80

Habakkuk
3:1, 81
3:3, 81
3:5–6, 81
3:9b–13a, 81
3:14–16a, 81
3:6, 48

Zephaniah
1:14–18, 121
3:17, 43

Zechariah
2:8, 82

9:9, 115, 119
10:3, 120
12:1, 71
14:9, 22, 131

Malachi
1:1, 71
2:7, 141
3:14, 105
3:18, 105

New Testament
Matthew
1:21, 124
2:6, 124
4:4, 9, 69
4:19, 71
6:9, 19
6:10, 120
6:23, 91
8:8b–9, 70
10:39, 102
11:21, 42
11:30, 104
13:22, 93, 105
16:13, 75
16:15, 75
18:20, 23
21:3, 52
21:43, 124
24:3, 122
24:15, 93
24:24, 136
28:20, 28

Mark
1:24, 98
2:2, 9
3:16, 18
5:41, 71
7:3, 71
12:1, 52
15:39, 130
16:20, 122

Luke
1:16, 33
1:35, 100
1:38, 74
1:45, 75
1:78, 120
2:10, 124
2:25, 117
2:37, 105
4:19, 9
5:20, 71
7:16, 120
11:10, 21
17:21, 115
17:24, 129
19:10, 120
19:38, 110
20:9, 52
22:19, 83
24:34, 130

John
general reference, 52
1:1, 67, 70
1:3, 67
1:4, 124
1:11, 120
1:14, 115
1:26, 2
1:43, 71
2:22, 115
3:6, 100
3:16, 105
3:21, 111
4:25b–26, 70
6:33, 115
6:63, 71
7:49, 136
8:56, 123
10:28, 124
10:34, 8
14:6, 83
12:28, 19
12:48, 69, 71

13:9, 69
13:19, 77
14:19, 105, 124
15:1, 43
15:3, 69
15:19, 105
17:6, 22
17:17, 97
17:19, 97
19:5, 111
21:16, 137

Acts
general reference, 135
1:8, 120
2:7–8, 60
2:11b, 60
2:17, 116
2:42, 13, 146
4:12, 22, 29, 32
5:5, 70
7, 52
7:37, 33
8:13, 122
8:30, 4
9:2, 84
12:24, 129
18:25, 84
19:9, 84
19:20, 9
19:23, 84

Romans
1:1, 71
4:11, 123
4:12, 77
4:17, 30, 70
5:20, 40
6:19, 93
7:6, 105
7:18, 100
8:3, 83
8:15, 32
8:16, 101
8:19, 115
8:27, 21
8:29, 51
8:29a, 30–31, 101
8:38–39, 24
9:25, 124
9:26, 71
9:28b, 82
11:33, 80
12:11, 105
14:7, 147
14:8, 105

1 Corinthians
1:2, 97
1:17, 141
3:17, 97
5:7, 123
6:2, 93
7:14, 93, 97
7:31, 106
11:24, 83
11:26, 83, 123
13:7, 8a, 55
13:12, 132
14:25, 130
15:37, 101

2 Corinthians
4:13, 75
4:17, 96
5:6, 85
5:8, 85
6:16, 124
9:4, 121
10:8, 121
13:12, 97

Galatians
4:26, 115
5:13, 71
5:20, 101

6:8, 100

Ephesians
1:18, 93
2:10, 112
3:15, 72
4:4, 71
4:9, 83
4:14, 144
5:14, 145
5:15, 17, 141
6:12, 93
6:13b, 6

Philippians
1:20, 121
3:3, 105
3:20b–21, 118

Colossians
1:12, 93
1:16, 66
1:19, 66
2:8, 83
3:24, 105

1 Thessalonians
2:14, 131
5:8, 119

1 Timothy
1:1, 119
4:4, 143
4:4–7, 14
4:7, 147
4:16, 14
6:11, 102
6:12, 71

2 Timothy
2:8, 83
2:23, 14
3:16, 10, 65

3:17, 111
4:7, 75

Hebrews
1:1–2a, 69
1:3, 69
2:1–3, 71
2:10–11, 97–98
3:10, 84
6:14, 130
8:10, 124
10:23, 118
11:10, 43, 118
12:9, 3
12:22, 115
13:12, 124

James
1:22, 75

1 Peter
1:3, 115
1:15, 71
1:16, 93
2:6, 121
2:9, 93, 102, 124
3:4, 111
3:15, 33
3:16, 121
4:16, 121
4:17, 136

2 Peter
3:13, 118

1 John
2:6, 112
2:15, 105
2:16, 93
3:2, 112
4:3, 55
4:8, 48
5:3, 104
5:20–21, 55

Revelation
1:4, 125
1:8, 33, 125
1:11, 126
2:17, 115
3:12, 115
3:20, 83
4:8, 33
5:6, 106
5:9, 125
5:11–12, 127
11:17, 33, 125
12:10, 115
14:1, 115
15:3, 33

16:7, 33
18:4, 124
19:7, 66
20:12, 87
21, 110
21:2, 10, 115
21:3, 115, 124
21:5–6, 80
21:6, 70, 126
21:22, 33
22:5, 33
22:13, 126
22:17, 74
22:20, 74, 115

Author Index

Barth, Karl, x, xvi, xxi–xxii, xxvn5, 5, 6n1, 145, 149n7
Bavinck, Herman, 44n2
Belgic Confession, 98
Bernard of Clairvaux, 51
Bloch, Ernst, xviii
Breukelman, Frans, xii, xivn4
Brod, Max, xviii, xx, xxvin12
Buber, Martin, xviii, xx

Calvin, John, 90
Childs, Brevard, x
Cleveringa, Rudolph P., xv, xxvn1
Cohen, Hermann, xviii

Da Costa, Isaac, 132n4
den Hertog, Niels, xvi
Drews, Arthur, 44n2
Deurloo, Karel, xii
de Vries, Jan, xxi, xxvin14
Doberstein, John, xii

Fichte, Johann Gottlieb, 67, 75n1

Goethe, Johann Wolfgang, 35
Green, Emma, xiiin1

Hammelsbeck, Oskar, 143, 145, 149n6, 149n8

Heidelberg Catechism, 14
Hellebroek, Abraham, 51, 55n2
Hielscher, Friedrich, xxi
Holst-Van der Schaik, Henriëtte Roland, xvii
Hugo, Victor, 35, 44n1
Husserl, Edmund, xix
Huxley, Aldous, 54

Janeff, Janko, xxi

Kafka, Franz, xviii
Kipling, Rudyard, 76n6
Klages, Ludwig, xxi
Kohlbrugge, H.F., xviii, xxvin9
Koopmans, Jan, xv, xxiii, xxvn2, xxvin16, 107n2

Leopold, J.H., 107n1, 107n3
Luther, Martin, 28, 33n1, 140

May, Karl, 87
Miskotte, K.H., xivn3, xivn5, xv–xvi, xviii–xix, xxi, xxiv, xxvn4, xxvn7, xxvin8, xxvinn10–11, xxvin13, xxvin15, xxvin17

Newman, John Henry, 135, 148n3
Nietzsche, Friedrich, 55n1

Noordmans, Oepke, xxiii

Origen of Alexandria, 51

Pius, X (Pope), 140–42, 149n5
Posner, Sarah, xiiin1

Rosenzweig, Franz, xiii, xvi, xviii, xx, 75–76n3, 132n1

Schelling, F.W.J., 132n1
Sertillanges, Antonin, 146, 149n9
Shakespeare, William, 35
Sidner, Sarah, xivn2
Simon, Mallory, xivn2

Spengler, Oswald, 66n2, 67, 75n2
Spinoza, Baruch, 21, 25n1
Steiner, Rudolf, 76n4
Stoevesandt, Hinrich, xi

't Hooft, Visser, xxiii

van der Meiden, Willem, xxvn6
van Rennes, Catharina, 33n2
van Roon, Ger, xxvn3

Watts, Isaac, 25n2

Ziegler, Leopold, xxi

About the Authors and Translators

Kornelis Heiko Miskotte (1894–1976), author of this work, was a pastor of the Dutch Reformed Church and a professor of dogmatics and ethics at the University of Leiden.

Rinse Reeling Brouwer, author of the introduction, is professor emeritus in the Miskotte/Breukelman chair for Biblical Hermeneutics at the Protestant Theological University, Amsterdam, the Netherlands.

Eleonora Hof (PhD, Protestant Theological University), translator, is pastor of Ieper/Ypres, United Protestant Church in Belgium.

Collin Cornell (PhD, Emory University), translator, is research affiliate and coordinator of the Center for Religion and Environment in the School of Theology at the University of the South in Sewanee, TN (USA).